ANIMALS ERASED

ANIMALS

DISCOURSE, ECOLOGY, AND

ERASED

RECONNECTION WITH THE NATURAL WORLD

ARRAN STIBBE

WESLEYAN UNIVERSITY PRESS Middletown, Connecticut

Wesleyan University Press
Middletown CT 06459
www.wesleyan.edu/wespress
2012 © Arran Stibbe
Manufactured in the United States of America
Designed by Vicki Kuskowski
Typeset in Van Dijck by Copperline Book Services, Inc.

Wesleyan University Press is a member of the Green Press Initiative. The
paper used in this book meets their minimum requirement for recycled paper.

The screenshot of the World Wildlife Fund website on page 69 is reproduced
with the permission of WWF (UK) from www.wwf.org.uk/what_we_do/safe
guarding_the_natural_world/wildlife/amur_leopard. Photograph of Amur
leopard © Vasily Solkin/WWF-Russia.

Library of Congress Cataloging-in-Publication Data
Stibbe, Arran.
Animals erased: discourse, ecology, and reconnection with the natural
world / Arran Stibbe.
    p. cm.
Includes bibliographical references and index.
ISBN 978-0-8195-7231-8 (cloth: alk. paper) —
ISBN 978-0-8195-7232-5 (paper: alk. paper) —
ISBN 978-0-8195-7233-2 (ebook)
1. Human-animal relationships.   2. Animals and civilization.
3. Animals—Social aspects.   4. Discourse analysis.   5. Animal
welfare.   6. Nature—Effect of human beings on.   7. Human
ecology—Philosophy.   8. Environmental ethics.   9. Ecology—
Philosophy.   10. Ecology—Moral and ethical aspects.   I. Title.
QL85.S795 2012
590—dc23   2011043352

5 4 3 2 1

Contents

Acknowledgments

This collection of essays represents ten years of research into relationships between humans and other animals. The chapters are based on articles that have been published by a wide range of peer-reviewed academic journals. Thanks are due to the publishers of these journals, all of whom have given permission to reuse material from the original articles in this book. Specifically, chapter 1 is based on Arran Stibbe, "Language, Power and the Social Construction of Animals," *Society and Animals* 9:2 (2001), with permission from the Society and Animals Forum. Chapter 2 is based on Arran Stibbe, "As Charming as a Pig: The Discursive Construction of the Relationship between Pigs and Humans," *Society & Animals* 11:4 (2003), with permission from the Society and Animals Forum. Chapter 3 is based on Arran Stibbe, "From Flu-like Virus to Deadly Disease: Ideology and the Media," *Journal of Media Psychology* 6:2 (2001), with permission from the Media Psychology Research Institute. Chapter 4 is based on Arran Stibbe, "Counter-discourses and Harmonious Relationships between Humans and other Animals, *Anthrozoös* 18:1 (2005), with the permission of the International Society for Anthrozoology. Chapter 5 is based on Arran Stibbe, "Deep Ecology and Language: The Curtailed Journey of the Atlantic Salmon," *Society and Animals* 14:1 (2006), with the permission of the Society and Animals Forum. Chapter 6 is based on Arran Stibbe and Francesca Zunino, "The Discursive Construction of Biodiversity," in Martin Döring, Hermine Penz, and Wilhelm Trampe (eds.), *Language, Signs and Nature: Ecolinguistic Dimensions of En-*

vironmental Discourse (Berlin: Stauffenburg Verlag, 2008), with permission from Stauffenburg Verlag and coauthor Francesca Zunino. Chapter 7 is based on Arran Stibbe, "Environmental Education across Cultures: Beyond the Discourse of Shallow Environmentalism," *Language & Intercultural Communication* 4:4 (2005), with permission from Taylor & Francis Ltd. Chapter 8 is based on Arran Stibbe, "Haiku and Beyond: Language, Ecology, and Reconnection with the Natural World, *Anthrozoös* 20:2 (2007), with the permission of the International Society for Anthrozoology. Chapter 9 is based on Arran Stibbe, "Zen and the Art of Environmental Education in the Japanese Animated Film *Tonari no Totoro*," *Journal for the Study of Religion, Nature and Culture* 1:4 (2007), with permission from Equinox Publishing (text from this chapter © Equinox Publishing Ltd., 2007). Thanks to Sarah Griffin and Julia Morris for invaluable help with proofreading. And finally thanks to Phil for his constant encouragement and assistance, and to Ryoko, Sen, and Kaya for being who they are.

ANIMALS ERASED

INTRODUCTION

VANISHING ANIMALS

Animals are disappearing, vanishing, dying out, not just in the physical sense of becoming extinct, but in the sense of being erased from our consciousness. Charles Bergman (2005) illustrates this in his description of ecologists who follow animals through jungles without ever catching a glimpse of them. Instead, they use a radio antenna to track the animals' movements:

> The animal with the radio-transmitter disappears as a visible, embodied creature. It emerges from its life into ours as a particular frequency on a receiver. While the radio-transmitter allows the animal to be followed and known in new ways and in new detail, the coded patterns of the beeps on the transmitter constitute signs of the creature's disappearance. (Bergman 2005: 257)

Increasingly, interactions with animals happen at a remove: animals are mediated by nature programs, books, magazines, the Internet, or cartoons; framed by the enclosures of zoos and aquariums; or exposed after death as exhibits in museums. John Berger (1980: 10) goes as far as stating that "In the last two centuries animals have gradually disappeared. Today we live without them." Berger's approach has been criticized in terms of historical detail and its lack of recognition for positive representations of animals (Burt 2005, Malamud 1998), but Burt does admit that

> the historical trajectory [Berger] outlines of the disappearance of animals and their replacement by signs, and the manner in which humans

and animals are increasingly alienated in modernity, provides a pessimistic vision with which it is hard to argue. (Burt 2005: 203)

When animals are erased, what we are left with are signs: words, pictures, toys, specimens, beeps on a radio receiver. Although the signs emerge at first with a connection to real animals, they can take on a life of their own in a simulated world, becoming what Jean Baudrillard (1994) calls "simulacra"—copies without an original. For instance, the happy speaking cows who advertise products made from their own bodies can be thought of as erasing the real animals:

> Advertisements' representations of "speaking animals" who are selling the end "products" of the brutal processes they endure in the factory farm system serve . . . a dual discursive purpose. The first purpose is to sell products, and the second role is . . . to make the nonhuman animal victims disappear. (Glenn 2004: 72)

Baudrillard (1994: 6) places images on a scale from the most direct representation toward a gradual disappearance of the referent:

- The image is the reflection of a profound reality.
- The image masks and denatures a profound reality.
- The image masks the absence of a profound reality.
- The image has no relation to any reality whatsoever: it is its own pure simulacrum.

While some images, representations, or simulacra may be benign, or even positive, there is a suspicion that slipping too far into a self-referential symbolic world has unexpected dangers. Abram (1996: 267) claims that "our organic atonement to the local earth is thwarted by our ever-increasing intercourse with our own signs," to the extent that we have become "so oblivious to the presence of other animals and the earth, that our current lifestyles and activities contribute daily to the destruction of whole ecosystems" (137).

Abram's claim is one of great importance, since it calls into question the idea that language, rationality, and the general ability to manipulate symbols form the core of what it means to be human because they are unique to humans.

In celebrating the linguistic and the rational, other aspects of being human (such as emotions, feelings, embodiment, mortality, or dependence on a physical environment for continued survival) are marginalized simply because they happen to be shared with other animals. By ignoring ecological embedding and embodiment, humans have managed to develop another unique characteristic: the ability, single-handedly as a species, to alter the conditions of the planet to make it less hospitable for human life and the life of countless other species. If we are to create a more humane and sustainable society, it will be necessary to look once again at animals and celebrate some of the characteristics that we share. This requires an understanding of the workings of the symbolic world — the mechanisms of erasure and alienation — in order to transcend the symbolic and reconnect with animals and the natural world.

Of particular concern for this book is the way that language is organized into *discourses*. Discourses, in the Foucaultian sense, are ways of speaking and writing that construct or shape the objects being spoken of. In other words, discourses are ways of speaking about the world that encode a particular model of reality. Stuart Hall (1997: 6) describes the concept of discourse as follows:

> Discourses are ways of referring to or constructing knowledge . . . a cluster . . . of ideas, images and practices, which provide ways of talking about, forms of knowledge and conduct associated with, a particular topic, social activity or institutional site in society.

The book investigates a wide range of discourses including those of animal industries, environmentalism, ecology, the animal rights movement, nature poetry, and Japanese animation. The main argument is that some "destructive" discourses represent animals in ways that promote inhumane treatment and environmental damage, that some "counter" discourses such as environmentalism fail to break free of the assumptions of destructive discourses, but that it is possible to discover radically different "alternative" discourses that encourage reconnection to animals and nature.

Underlying the activity of critical discourse analysis is the hope of change — that if discourses construct society along inhumane or unsustainable lines, then it might be possible to discover and promote discourses that encourage more harmonious relations with animals and the natural world. Although alternative discourses are still representations, they could provide "an image of a profound reality" (in Baudrillard's terms) rather than a "simulacrum," and encourage readers to interact more directly with the natural world simply by encouraging them to lift their eyes from the page and view the world in a new way. In other words, discourses have the power to erase animals or work against the forces of erasure.

It is important from the outset to distinguish discourse analysis from an approach that is narrowly prescriptive about the specific linguistic forms that people *should* use when talking about animals. Smith-Harris (2004: 15), for instance, suggests that if people stopped using the expression "euthanizing companion animals" and instead talked about 'killing cats and dogs by lethal injection because no one wanted them," then it would make it harder to accept violent acts toward animals. She describes how "eating pâté sounds refined, whereas eating the swollen liver of a force-fed goose sounds quite different." Dunayer (2001) similarly recommends avoiding the terms *beast, aquarium,* and *dairy farmer* and replacing them with *nonhuman animal, aquaprison,* and *cow enslaver* respectively (188, 191, 194). Other terms that Dunayer suggests are *free-living nonhumans* instead of *wildlife* (189), *genocide by hunting* for *overhunting* (190), *food-industry captive* for *farm animal* (193) and *cattle abuser* for *cowboy* (194).

The problem with being prescriptive about individual terms like this, however, is that it provides only one "politically correct" way of speaking and closes down options for creatively redefining the world along new lines. We have already learned, from the area of sexism, that "language campaigns have been made problematic . . . because of . . . ridiculing of any attempts to reform or call for change" (Mills 2003: 90). As Fairclough (2003b: 25) points out, " 'Political correctness' and being 'politically correct' are identifications imposed upon people by their political opponents [providing] a remarkably effective way of disorientating sections of the left." That is not to say that the negativity surrounding political correctness is entirely undeserved, since, as Fairclough goes on to say, "some (but only some) discursive intervention smacked of the arrogance, self-righteousness and Puritanism of an ultra-left politics, and [has] caused widespread resentment even among people basically committed to anti-racism, anti-sexism, etc." (25).

Any attempt to suggest that the expression *swollen liver of a force-fed goose* should be used in general discourse instead of *pâté*, or *food industry captive* be used instead of *farm animal* could be met with ridicule, and the larger project of discursive change summarily dismissed. Mills (2003: 90) concludes that "any anti-sexist language campaign . . . has to define itself in contradistinction to what has been defined as 'political correctness' by the media," and discursive analysis of animals may need to do likewise.

The approach of critical discourse analysis (Fairclough 2003a) is particularly effective in moving beyond the limitations of political correctness. Rather than judging the merit of individual expressions or linguistic devices in isolation, a discourse approach analyzes the way that linguistic features *cluster together* to model the world in particular ways. For example, animal industry discourses use the pronoun *it* to refer to animals, use expressions that represent animals as machines, use the passive to hide the agent of killing, and use a range of other features that combine together to model a world where animals are constructed as objects. A political correctness approach would try to ban or proscribe particular expressions or grammatical features such as the use of the passive or the pronoun *it* when speaking of animals. A discourse approach, on the other hand, would recognize that it is particular *combinations* of features that create models of the world. So the use of the pronoun *it* in industry texts may be part of a discourse that objectifies animals, but the same pronoun could be used as part of a quite different discourse of empathy and respectful distance, as in the following passage:

> I stepped out from a clutch of trees and found myself looking into the
> face of one of the rare and beautiful bison that exist only on that island.
> Our eyes locked. When it snorted, I snorted back; when it lifted its
> shoulders, I shifted my stance; when I tossed my head, it tossed *its* head

in reply. I found myself caught in a nonverbal conversation with this Other. (Abram 1996: 21)

Cultures and societies are structured by a range of dominant discourses used in particular industries, academic disciplines, governments, charities, media, institutions, and everyday life. This book uses the term *destructive discourses* for discourses that potentially construct inhumane and ecologically damaging relationships between humans and animals. Dunayer (2001) analyzes a wide range of discourses including the discourse of zoos, science, hunting, the meat industry, and aquariums, showing how the language used by these institutions constructs animals as unfeeling objects ready for human oppression. Since destructive discourses are so much a part of mainstream ways of thinking and talking about the world, they can go unnoticed and just be treated as "the way things are." Analysis of such discourses can expose and critique the models of the world that they are based on, and act as a first step toward opening up alternatives.

OVERVIEW OF THE BOOK

Chapters 1 and 2 both begin by exploring destructive discourses within *general* discourse, that is, ways of talking about animals that are in common usage across a wide range of contexts and situations in everyday life. There are a significant number of expressions within general discourse that represent animals negatively. The "pig" in expressions like *greedy pig, sweating like a pig, dirty pig*, and *stubborn pig* is far down on Baudrillard's scale of representations. Expressions such as these do more than "mask and denature a profound reality"; the disgusting creature created is a simulacrum, existing only in the world of discourse and not in reality, where real pigs despise being dirty, do not sweat, and are stubborn only in the sense of not always doing what humans want them to.

Jepson (2008) describes another way that general discourse represents animals negatively in her study of how killing is lexicalized in the case of humans and animals. She observes how the word *slaughter*, when applied to animals, contains no moral evaluation, whereas when applied to humans it carries a connotation of a despicable act. This, and other evidence, leads her to conclude that general discourse encodes a model where "the detached, impassive killing of cows, chickens, turkeys, or pigs is accepted. . . . However, applying that impassivity to the killing of humans is despicable" (Jepson 2008: 144). Smith-Harris (2004) similarly investigates animal idioms such as "the straw that broke the camel's back," and "flogging a dead horse," concluding that "negative animal idioms, metaphors and euphemisms are pervasive and indicate that there is a societal permissiveness to implied cruelty toward nonhuman animals" (12).

There are limitations, however, in analyzing "general" English discourse. As Bakhtin points out, the idea of there being one coherent national language like "English" is a myth in the same way as the idea of "English culture" is (Dentith 1995). Instead there is a multiplicity of different varieties of language used by different groups in society, representing multiple and different ways of modelling the world. The language used to describe animals in a Disney documentary is quite different from that of a slaughterhouse instruction manual. Discourses therefore need to be analyzed separately so that the different models of the world they are based on can be exposed. Chapter 1 moves on from the starting point of analyzing general discourse to look at the clustering of language features within the specific discourses of animal product industries.

Chapter 2 focuses on one particular animal product industry for detailed investigation. The chapter reveals how the discourse of intensive pig farming uses metaphors, pronouns, definitions, presuppositions, and other linguistic techniques to represent pigs as objects, machines, inanimate resources, variables, and as a mass rather than as individuals. To borrow the words of Adams (1993: 201), within the discourse of the pork industry "someone who has a very particular, situated life, a unique being, is converted into something that has no distinctiveness, no uniqueness, no individuality." The discourse justifies a system of farming that treats pigs in ways that go against their nature, causing immense suffering as well as environmental damage.

The analysis of the language of animal product industries in chapters 1 and 2 comes to much the same conclusions as Glenn's (2004) research. Glenn found that within the internal industry discourse of factory farms, "nonhuman animals are constructed . . . as objects and commodities whose only value is as product to be used or consumed by human animals" (Glenn 2004: 76). On the other hand, within the external industry discourse (e.g., advertising and press releases) "an assortment of corporate strategies have ensued that construct an image of a benevolently beneficial industry" (64). In this way, "factory farm industry discourse helps construct how US Americans think about animals in ways that—tacitly and oftentimes unintentionally—endorse industry practices even in the face of serious concerns raised by environmental and animal advocates" (76). This has important consequences since "the evidence is overwhelming that factory farms are hazardous to the environment" (76).

The discourses of the animal product industries have an impact that goes well beyond the United States, however. They are part of globalized discourses spread across the world by transnational corporations (Stibbe 2009). More than simply "endorsing industry practices" (Glenn 2004: 76), industry discourses are the blueprint for those practices. They provide a model of the world where animals are constructed as components in a system of mass production, and as these discourses spread they reproduce the practices—of mass production—wherever they go. Smithfield Foods, for example, is a huge transnational company that has received criticism for bringing both the discourse and the practice of intensive pig farming to Poland on a huge scale (Deutsch 2005).

Chapter 3 explores media discourse, looking specifically at the portrayal of foot-and-mouth disease in the British press. Although this chapter provides just a single case study, the findings are consistent with the larger pattern of representation of animals in the media discovered by Freeman (2009). Freeman begins by describing the important role of the media in representing farmed animals. So much intensive farming goes on behind closed doors that often media representations provide the only source of information that the public gets. At stake is whether animals "are publicly defined and treated as sentient beings in need of justice or as mere commodities for continued use" (79). Through study of an extensive corpus of U.S. media texts, Freeman discovers that animals are overwhelmingly portrayed as commodities. He notes that the media fail to consider animals' perspectives or emotions; they construct animals as bodies, not beings; and they express the negative impacts of factory farms in terms of the damage to people's health rather than the ordeal suffered by the animals. This is because news organizations "operate within a network of other powerful institutions in society — such as corporations, [and] governmental agencies" (84), and these institutions may be acting to serve short-term financial or political interests. Freeman (97) argues that "while no story explicitly states 'the interests of farmed animals do not matter,' on the whole, the news implicitly states this as a rule of discourse by failing to address the animals' feelings, perspectives, or emotions in most stories."

Chapters 4, 5, and 6 explore what the book calls *counter-discourses*. Counter-discourses are mainstream discourses that explicitly aim to promote animal welfare or rights, ameliorate environmental destruction, conserve wildlife, or protect ecosystems. The movements that these discourses arise from are clearly important in dealing with some of the unintended impacts of destructive discourses, such as the environmental destruction and suffering caused by intensive farming. However, the movements themselves spring from a society where instrumentalist worldviews that objectify animals and deny their intrinsic worth are deeply entrenched. The question is whether the counter-discourses manage to transcend and provide alternatives to destructive discourses, or whether they are based on similar assumptions. Plumwood (2003: 3) describes how

> ecology . . . often retains the human-centred resource view of animals and scientistic resistance to seeing animals as individuals with life stories of attachment, struggle and tragedy not unlike our own, refusing to apply ethical thinking to the nonhuman sphere.

Indeed, chapters 4 and 5 describe the extraordinary lengths that some counter-discourses go to in order to avoid treating animals as living beings, referring to them, for instance, as "biotic components of ecosystems." Chapter 6 focuses in on one term that is frequently used in counter-discourses, *biodiversity*, investigating the complex pattern of different senses of the term. On the one hand, *biodiversity* can be used to describe a fundamental property of healthy ecosystems and to argue for protection of those ecosystems, but it can also be used more trivially to argue for conservation of token numbers of rare species in zoos.

The critique of environmental discourse is taken to a global level in chapter 7, which looks at environmental textbooks written by Western authors specifically for use in Japan. These textbooks, while ostensibly promoting environmental messages, seem to simultaneously convey images of animals as objects or resources, despite traditions in Japan of respect for nature. If counter-discourses fail to transcend the assumptions of an unsustainable society that instrumentalizes animals and nature then, in the end, they can only play a role in what James Allen calls "fighting against circumstances":

> What, then, is the meaning of "fighting against circumstances"? It means that a man is continuously revolting against an *effect* without, while all the time he is nourishing and preserving its *cause* in his heart (Allen 1951: 19)

It could be argued that the current trajectory that society is on is so clearly heading toward ecological collapse and that intensive farms are damaging animals' welfare on such a huge scale that we need to do more than fight against circumstances. What is needed is a larger shift of consciousness, a change in dominant models of reality and the discourses that encode them.

This book uses the term *alternative discourses* to refer to discourses that are based on very different assumptions from both the destructive and counter-discourses of mainstream society. Ideally, they are discourses that represent humans as both part of and dependent on natural systems, encourage respect for animals and the natural world, and promote the fulfilling of human needs in ways that do not destroy the ecosystems that support life. The Earth Charter provides an example of an alternative discourse along these lines. The Charter explicitly encourages the reader to "recognise that all beings are interdependent and every form of life has value regardless of its worth to human beings." More than that, though, it uses language in a way that is consistent with this viewpoint. The Charter talks of, for example, "the Earth community," "the greater community of life," "a unique community of life," "a magnificent diversity of cultures and lifeforms," and the "joyful celebration of life" (Newman 2009: 101). In all these expressions, humans, animals and other life-forms are treated equally as part of the same community. This is quite different from mainstream environmentalism, which sets up a binary distinction between humans and "the environment"—animals usually being only a part of the "environment."

The eccentric writings of William Hedgepeth provide an example of another alternative discourse—a highly original way of representing pigs. Hedgepeth uses psychological and spiritual discourse, along with a large dose of humor, to represent pigs as beings of great depth:

> Various breeds [of pig] may shine forth in one regard or another, may be personable, courageous, droll, often profound in subtle philosophical ways, and certainly far brainier than most other domestic or even household beasts. . . . Few [farmers] fail to sense the vast, untapped potentialities of the hog, or fail to perceive the strange glow of awe that fills their minds when they think about it. (Hedgepeth 1998: 59–60)

The model of pigs that this discourse encodes lies in stark opposition to mainstream discourses that, in Hedgepeth's words, model pigs along the lines of "any obscenely rotund beast with a tropism for mud who trundles filthily along oinking" (Hedgepeth 1998, 21). That is not to suggest for a moment that, in a politically correct way, everyone "should" use language in the same way as Hedgepeth. Hedgepeth's discourse will appeal to some and encourage them to think of pigs in a new way, with more respect, but will not appeal to others. Instead, what is important is the creativity Hedgepeth uses in challenging mainstream discourse, demonstrating that reality can be modeled in quite different ways but not trumpeting that his particular way is the only correct one.

In the search for discourses that are based on very different assumptions from mainstream destructive discourses and counter-discourses of the West, it makes sense to stretch across time and space and draw insights from traditional cultures around the world. Chapters 8 and 9 explore alternative discourses drawn from traditional Japanese culture. The author spent eight years in rural Japan analyzing language and at the same time gaining practical experience of the traditional culture and ecology of Japan, and the analyses draw from this experience.

One of the most important strands within the philosophies of Japan is a suspicion of the power of the symbolic world to erase the more immediate and sensually based reality. The concerns over erasure expressed in postmodern continental philosophy have been a theme within Eastern traditions such as Tao and Zen from long ago. D. T. Suzuki (1970: 5) wrote:

> Zen is not necessarily against words, but is well aware of the fact that they are always liable to detach themselves from realities and turn into conceptions. And this conception is what Zen is against.

Zen has influenced a great number of traditional discourses in Japan, from the discourse of the tea ceremony, haiku poetry, traditional crafts, and martial arts to everyday language. The influence points in the direction of simplicity, flowing with nature, and experiencing direct and unmediated interaction with reality. Japan is particularly good at keeping its traditions alive at the sidelines of mainstream culture, even if the prevailing economic expansionist ideology has proven to be ecologically destructive.

Chapter 8 explores in detail how one Zen-inspired discourse, that of haiku nature poetry, represents relationships between humans, animals, and the natural world. The haiku poems in this discourse record a momentary yet profound connection between the author and the natural world, and attempt to represent it in as direct and unembellished a way as possible. In other words, they appear at the top of Baudrillard's (1994: 6) scale, providing "the reflection of a profound reality." The reality they represent is one of common animals as active agents leading their own lives for their own purposes, with the observer respecting and valuing the life of the other without interference. The poems describe insights into what it means to be alive through close observations of others who share the same cycle of birth and death, and celebrate similarity with animals rather than difference. Above all, haiku describe an embodied and ecologically embedded view of the world that could encourage people to learn from natural systems rather than attempt to conquer them.

Chapter 9 describes how a discourse similar to that of haiku has emerged within animated films, a medium that has the potential of reaching a much wider international audience than haiku poetry. The chapter explores how one particular film, *Tonari no Totoro*, weaves together the natural with the supernatural and sacred to express the intrinsic value of nature. Although the film is a form of representation, and can therefore never accurately portray direct experience of interacting with the natural world, what it does do is to *model* ways of engaging with the local natural environment that viewers may (or may not) adopt in their own lives after watching the film. Like haiku, the model is one of direct and respectful interaction with animals and plants, rather than with symbols or conceptions of them.

As the impact of climate change and peak oil makes itself increasingly felt and the current system of food and energy production becomes less able to support the needs of humanity, alternative models of society and reality will be urgently sought. The conclusion of the book argues that there has never been a more important time to critically analyze the dominant discourses of unsustainable societies and seek alternatives that provide radically different models of the relationship between humans, animals, and the natural world.

METHODOLOGICAL AND PHILOSOPHICAL CONSIDERATIONS

The idea that discourses can be objectively classified into categories of *destructive* (e.g., animal industry discourses), *counter* (e.g., the discourse of environmentalism), or *alternative* (e.g., haiku) just by analyzing them is, of course, a simplification. There is no fixed algorithm for deciding whether a discourse is likely to encourage people to behave in ecologically destructive ways. What can be done, to a greater or lesser extent, however, is to expose the underlying models of the world that particular discourses assume to be the case. These can be compared with the analyst's own philosophy of relationships between humans, animals, plants and the physical environment—an *ecosophy* to use Naess's (1990) term. For instance, if the analyst's ecosophy is based on the importance of recognizing animals as being worthy of moral consideration beyond their usefulness to humans, then discourse can be analyzed critically on how hidden messages embedded within it deny or affirm intrinsic worth.

It could be argued that this is merely comparing the models in the discourses under consideration with the favored models of the analyst. That is, in fact, exactly what all critical analysis consists of—the analyst has an ideal model of, say, a nonracist or equal society and analyzes dominant discourse to expose hidden oppressive ideology that is incompatible with that goal. The difference here is that the models being used take into consideration relationships between humans and the natural world (which many social science models do not) and that the models of the analyst are, as far as possible, made explicit.

The ecosophy that this book is based on evolves gradually over the chapters, since the chapters consist of separate but related essays written over the course of ten years. At first, the ecosophy merely extends the central concern of critical discourse analysis (oppression and exploitation of some people by other people) to the oppression of animals by humans. After all, as van Dijk (1993: 252) points out, a primary criterion of the work of a critical discourse analyst is "solidarity with those who need it most. Their problems are real problems, that is, the serious problems that threaten the lives or well-being of many." Those who need solidarity most undoubtedly include the millions, or billions, of animals suffering in intensive farming industries and lacking a voice to protest about their treatment.

The ecosophy of oppression is only part of the story, however, and as Burt (2005: 204) argues, "we should be careful not to collapse the kinds of analyses used to understand human-human relationships onto human-animal relations." In particular it is important not to represent humans as simply *gaining benefit* from the exploitation of animals. Incarcerating animals in intensive farming systems, destroying habitats such as forests and oceans, and polluting the environment that animals live in not only oppresses animals, it also undermines the ecological systems that human life depends on.

The case of pigs provides a suitable illustration of this. In a natural environment, pigs pull straw around them to keep warm, cool down in the mud, and root around for food; meanwhile their waste fertilizes surrounding vegetation. When they are treated in ways that go against their nature and are kept in their thousands indoors, then it becomes necessary to use artificial fertilizers and pesticides to grow their food, energy to heat and cool their housing, and drugs to control disease. There are also large quantities of polluting waste produced. This is both environmentally damaging and unsustainable, particularly since oil production is about to peak and begin its inevitable decline, threatening the supply of fertilizers, pesticides, and energy. In general, when animals are treated in ways that go grossly against their nature, the results are damaging not only for the animals but also for the ecological systems that support human life. Or put more positively, if animals are treated in ways that better accord with their nature, then this can contribute to more sustainable human societies.

The ecosophy therefore evolves over the chapters to include more ecological elements until it arrives at a point where it is close to Plumwood's (2003) *Ecological Animalism*. Plumwood argues that abuse of animals and ecosystems is

> enabled and justified by a dominant human-centred ideology of mastery over an inferior sphere of animals and nature. It is this ideology that is expressed in economies that treat commodity animals reductively as less than they are, as a mere human resource, little more than living meat or egg production units. (Plumwood 2003: 1)

The framework that Plumwood (2003: 2) suggests as an alternative to dominant ideologies "supports and celebrates animals and encourages a dialogical ethics of sharing and negotiation or partnership between humans and animals, while undertaking a re-evaluation of human identity that affirms inclusion in animal and ecological spheres."

Plumwood argues that it is possible to make use of animals and plants without having to mentally construct them as inferior beings or worthless objects first. The idea of "respectful use" transcends the binary veganist notion of "no use under any circumstances," which has nothing to say about the difference between, for example, intensive factory farming and organic permaculture.

Respectful use implies using animals minimally, always thinking of them and treating them as *more than* the products or services they provide for humans, as well as being grateful for those services.

Recognition of the ecological embedding of humans is essential if humans are to do what other animals do quite naturally when left to themselves—survive and thrive without using vast subsidies of energy from fossil fuels and without producing masses of contamination and pollution. Plumwood's framework implies a shift of consciousness and priorities toward allowing the animals that we do use to live according to their nature as far as possible, letting animals in the wild fulfill their roles within the ecosystems that support life, celebrating aspects of being human that are shared with other animals, and learning from animals about how to live sustainably. The framework demands the recognition that the future of humans is not in competition with the future of other animals—that either we all survive together within a thriving web of life, or humans as well as countless other species face at best a grim future and at worst no future at all.

This ecosophy, in its different stages from oppression to ecological animalism, is used in the analysis of language in each chapter. The aim is to use linguistic techniques to expose the models of the world that particular discourses are based on and then measure those models against the ecosophy, pointing out where they fall short of the ecosophical principles. For instance, the ecosophy places great emphasis on respecting the nature of animals, and discourses are criticized for denying that nature and representing them as machines or objects.

Overall, the argument of this book is that the discourses we use to construct our conceptions of animals and nature have important consequences for the well-being of the animals and the ecosystems that support life. As dominant models spread across the world under the forces of globalization, they contribute to increasing levels of ecological destruction and suffering. These discourses need to be challenged, but not on the rather petty level of proscribing and prescribing individual linguistic features. Instead, space needs to be opened up for a wide range of alternative discourses that are based on very different models of the world.

Baker (2001: xvi) feels that "it should not simply be a matter of our studying what animals already signify in the culture but rather, through a benevolent manipulation, of exploring what animals might yet be *made to signify*." Calarco (2008) goes further, demanding "the revolution in language and thought that is needed to come to grips with the issues surrounding animal life." He claims that "There is no doubt that we need to think unheard-of thoughts about animals, that we need new languages, new artworks, new histories even new sciences and philosophies." It is to the search for "new languages," or rather "new discourses," that this is book is dedicated.

1

Destructive Discourses

ANIMALS WITHIN A SYMBOLIC WORLD

Fairclough (1992b: 2) describes the "linguistic turn" in social theory, where toward the end of the twentieth century language began to be "accorded a more central role within social phenomena." The role of language in structuring power relations, in particular, has come under close scrutiny (van Dijk 1997, Fairclough 1989, Hodge and Kress 1993, Fowler 1991). Most of this work on language and power focuses on the role of discourse in oppression and exploitation. For example, the journal *Discourse and Society* is dedicated to "power, dominance and inequality, and to the role of discourse in their legitimisation and reproduction in society, for instance in the domains of gender, race, ethnicity, class or world religion" (van Dijk 2000). However, with rare exceptions, the role of discourse in the domination by humans of other species has been almost entirely neglected in the field of critical discourse analysis. Power is talked about as if it is a relation between people only; for example, Fairclough (1992b: 64) describes the way that "language contributes to the domination of some *people* by others" (emphasis added).

One of the main reasons that animals tend to be excluded from discussions of language and power is that they cannot use language to resist how they have been discursively constructed. Because of the neo-Marxist roots of critical discourse analysis, analysis focuses on hegemony, where oppression of a group is carried out ideologically rather than coercively, through the manufacture of consent (Fairclough 1992b: 92). In the case of animals, the power is coercive, carried out by a small number of people involved in organizations that farm and use animals. The animals do not consent to their treatment because of an uncritical acceptance of the ideology of the oppressor, and they cannot be empowered to resist the discourses that oppress them.

However, the coercive power used to oppress animals depends on the consent of the majority of the human population, who explicitly or implicitly agree to the way animals are treated every time they buy animal products. This consent can be withdrawn, as has been demonstrated through boycotts of veal, battery farm eggs, cosmetics tested on animals, and, by some, all animal products. It is in the manufacturing of consent within the human population for the oppression and exploitation of animals that language plays a role.

Shotter (1993) uses the term "rhetorical-responsive" to describe the way that social constructions exist not in the minds of individual people but within the constant interaction and exchange of information in a society. There is what Kopperud (1993: 20) calls "a pitched battle for the hearts and minds of . . . consumers" taking place between the meat industry and animal rights activists, a struggle that occurs primarily through language and the media. Jones (1997: 73), for example, found that "public opposition to both the use of animals in scientific research and the killing of animals for fur increased significantly following the high level of media coverage given."

The way that animals are socially constructed influences how they are treated by human society: as Lawrence (1994: 182) puts it, "cultural constructs determine the fate of animals." These "cultural constructs" are intimately bound up with language and discourse. According to Fairclough (1992b: 64), discourse "is a practice not just of representing the world, but of signifying the world, constituting and constructing the world in meaning."

Van Dijk (1997) considers the link between discourse and society to be through ideology and social cognition. One of the classic senses of ideology is a mode of thought and practice "developed by dominant groups in order to reproduce and legitimate their domination" (25). The primary way that this is accomplished is to present domination as "God-given, natural, benign [or] inevitable (25). Rather than explicitly encouraging oppression and exploitation, ideology manifests itself more effectively by being implicit. This is achieved by basing discourse on assumptions that are treated as if they were common sense, but which are, in fact, "common sense assumptions in the service of sustaining unequal relations of power" (Fairclough 1989: 84).

Ideologies, embedded and disseminated through discourse, influence the individual mental representations of members of a society, which in turn influence their actions. These mental representations are part of what Van Dijk (1997: 27) calls "social cognition," since they are shared among members of a society through participation in and exposure to discourse. In the end, it is this social cognition that influences which animal products people buy, how the meat industry treats animals, and whether people actively campaign against the oppression of animals.

Animals play many roles in human society, including the roles of companion, entertainer, food item, and commodity. There are therefore numerous discourses and ideologies that influence how they are socially constructed. The emphasis in this chapter is on discourses that have a direct impact on the welfare of large numbers of animals, starting with general discourse but focusing particularly on discourses used in animal product industries.

The data that this chapter examines are based on a corpus collected from a variety of different sources, all of which were publicly available and therefore potentially influential. The corpus consists of: (a) articles from "internal" meat industry magazines such as *Poultry* and *Meat Marketing & Technology* (MM&T), (b) articles written by the meat industry for external reading, for example, justifying farming methods, and (c) professional articles written by interested parties such as veterinarians specializing in food animals or lawyers involved in the defense of product manufacturers. In addition to the specialist discourses that appear in the corpus, general discourse is also discussed. The term *general discourse* is used to mean terms and expressions that are used widely across a range of discourses in everyday life rather than being associated with particular groups. The data for this come from personal observation and consultation of general dictionaries, idiom dictionaries, and grammar books.

The method used to analyze the data is a form of critical discourse analysis (CDA) (Chilton and Schäffner 1997, Van Dijk 1993, Fairclough 1992b), combined with Potter's (1996) theory of fact construction. CDA provides "an account of the role of language, language use, discourse or communicative events in the (re)production of dominance and inequality" (Van Dijk 1993: 282). It does this by performing detailed linguistic analysis of discourses to expose the ideologies embedded within them. Chilton and Schäffner (1997: 226) provide an explicit methodology for CDA, aimed at "interpretively linking linguistic details . . . to the strategic political functions of coercion, resistance, opposition, protest, dissimulation, legitimisation and delegitimisation." The methodology they present echoes that of Fairclough (1992b, 1989) in focusing on the analysis of linguistic features such as vocabulary, grammar, textual structures, and punctuation in order to reveal hidden ideological assumptions on which discourse is based.

This process of revealing "commonsense" assumptions can be important because, as Fairclough (1989: 85) writes, "If one becomes aware that a particular aspect of common sense is sustaining power inequalities at one's own expense, it ceases to *be* common sense, and may cease to have the capacity to sustain power inequalities." Clearly, in this case, the commonsense assumptions are sustaining power inequalities at the expense of animals, but given the ecologically destructive nature of intensive farming and the many ways that humans depend on other animals for our continuing survival, discourses that condone inhumane or destructive practices toward animals have an ultimate impact on humans too.

The following discussion, based on detailed analysis of the data mentioned above, is aimed at answering the following question: How does language, from the level of pragmatics and semantics down to syntax and morphology, influence the way that animals are socially constructed, and hence treated, by human society, in general discourse as well as the discourse of animal products industries? The answer to this question is necessarily brief but taken up in more detail in chapter 2

GENERAL DISCOURSE

Singer (1990/1975: vi) describes the way that "the English language, like other languages, reflects the prejudices of its users." The example he gives is of the word *animal*, which, in contrast to its use in scientific discourse, often excludes human beings from its semantic extension. It is quite usual to talk about "animals and people," or to say "there are no animals here" when there are, in fact, people. This semantic classification could potentially contribute to oppression by reproducing "outgroup social psychology . . . which distances us from, and prevents us from seeing, animal suffering" (Shapiro 1995: 671).

Other linguistic mechanisms that distance us from animal suffering occur at the lexical level: "The very words we use conceal its [meat's] origin, we eat beef, not bull . . . and pork, not pig" (Singer 1990/1975: 95). We also wear leather made from *hide*, not skin, and eat a *carcass*, not a corpse. As Shapiro (1995: 671) points out "We do not say 'please pass the cooked flesh'": meat is meat, with quite different connotations from circumlocutions with the same meaning such as "bits of the dead bodies of animals." The shock value of such circumlocutions was exploited by the BBC news during the "BSE crisis" when reporting the fact that cattle were being fed "mashed up cows." Killing, too, is lexicalized differently for humans and animals: animals are slaughtered, humans are murdered. Interchanging these two: "You murdered my pet hamster" is comical, "The refugees were slaughtered" means they were killed brutally, uncaringly, and immorally.

Animals are not only represented in language as different, but also as inferior, the two conditions necessary for oppression. Conventional metaphors, which Lakoff and Johnson (1999, 1980) claim have a strong influence on our everyday thinking, are overwhelmingly negative to animals. For example, a person might be called a "greedy pig," "dirty dog," "stupid cow," "big ape," or "ugly bitch" or be criticized for acting "catty," "crowing" over achievements, being "chicken," or "monkeying" around (see Leach 1964; Palmatier 1995). Such terms contain nouns, adjectives, and verbs that have become polysemous through metaphorical extension in ways negative toward animals.

Idioms that refer to animals also tend to describe negative situations, or contain images of cruelty. There are various expressions about dogs: "sick as a dog," "dying like a dog," "dog's dinner," "it's a dog's life," "working like a dog," "going to the dogs." And cats: "cat on hot bricks," "not enough room to swing a cat," "a cat in hell's chance," "running like a scalded cat," "many ways to skin a cat." And larger animals: "flogging a dead horse," "the straw that broke the camel's back," "talking the hind legs off a donkey." The only positive animal idioms seem to be idioms describing wild birds and insects, for example: "an early bird," "in fine feather," "feathering your nest," "being as free as a bird," "happy as a lark," "wise as an owl," and "snug as a bug in a rug," "chirpy as a cricket," "as fit as a flea," "the bee's knees." There are exceptions to this pattern, but the pattern is clear: the closer the relation of dominance of a particular species by humans, the more negative the stereotypes contained in the idioms of general discourse.

The ideological positioning of animals extends into syntax as well. When animals die they change from being objects to substance, count nouns to mass nouns, in a way that humans do not. It is quite possible to say "some chicken," "some lamb," or "some chicken leg," but "some human" and "some human leg" are ungrammatical. Singer (1990/1975: 95) is surprised that while we disguise the origin of pig meat by calling it pork, we "find it easier to face the true nature of a leg of lamb." However, there is a clear grammatical difference here: we cannot say "a leg of person," instead we say "a person's leg." Expressing the lamb example similarly (e.g., "Tonight we are going to eat a lamb's leg") does not hide the origin in the same way.

Another place where animals change from count nouns to mass nouns is on safari. Whether the participants are carrying guns or cameras, the way of talking about animals is the same: "We saw giraffe, elephant, and lion," instead of "We saw giraffes, elephants, and lions." Using mass nouns instead of count nouns removes the individuality of the animals, with the ideological assumption that each animal is just a (replaceable) representative of a category. Lawrence (1994: 180) writes, "If there are no differences among members of a group, their value and importance are greatly diminished so that it is easier to dislike them and to justify their exploitation and destruction."

Pronoun use can lead to the kind of "us" and "them" division similar to that found in racist discourse, with "us" referring to humans and "them" to animals. Even in the animal rights literature the pronouns *we, us,* and *our* are almost always used exclusively, that is, referring only to humans. Perhaps the strongest animal rights campaigner of all, Tom Regan (1996: 37), writes, "We want and prefer things . . . our enjoyment and suffering . . . make[s] a difference to the quality of our lives as lived . . . by us as individuals." This appears to be an inclusive use of *us, we,* and *our,* until the next sentence is read: "The same is true of . . . animals."

The common way of referring to animals as "it" rather than "him" or "her" can objectify them when used in certain contexts. Objects can be "bought," "sold," and "owned," a lexical set used routinely in everyday conversation when talking about animals. This reveals the "commonsense" assumption that animals are property. It is semantically deviant to talk about someone "owning" another human, unless the term is used metaphorically, where it refers to immoral and unfair domination.

Spender's (1998) book *Man Made Language* shows how general discourse, evolving in a male-oriented society, both reflects and reproduces bias against women. In the same way, it is not surprising to find that general discourse reflects negative attitudes toward animals. The extent to which this influences people to condone exploitation is uncertain, but general discourse is reinforced by the discourses of groups that have commercial interests in justifying inhumane and environmentally damaging ways of treating animals.

THE DISCOURSE OF THE ANIMAL PRODUCT INDUSTRIES

One type of ideology, as mentioned above, presents oppression as being "God-given, natural, benign, [or] inevitable" (van Dijk 1997: 25). Oppression of animals is often justified quite literally as sanctioned by God through the much-quoted verse from Genesis (1:28) where God gives humans "dominion" over animals. The animal product industry, however, does not use the discourse of religion. Instead the discourse of science, among others, is used to make oppression appear natural and inevitable (see Sperling 1988).

The discourse of evolutionary biology is often invoked to equate the intensive farming and slaughter of animals with the behavior of predators in the wild, representing it as "natural." Linguistic devices are used to accomplish this, as can be seen in the article "The Natural Wrongs about Animal Rights and Animal Liberation," by Randall S. Ott, a specialist in the industry-related field of bovine reproduction.

After explicitly declaring that "people are animals," Ott's (1995) article uses collocations such as "the human animal," and "animals other than human beings" (1023–24) to emphasize a semantic classification in which, unlike general discourse, humans are included in the category "animals." He also includes humans in the semantic category of "predator":

> The natural relationship between predator and prey is congruent with neither an egalitarian nor an animal rights viewpoint. . . . Predator-prey relationships and a hierarchical utilisation of other beings, alive and dead, is essential to nature. (Ott 1995: 1024)

This treats as "common sense" the assumption that what applies to the (non-human) animal situation of predation is the same as that which applies to the human situation. However, prototypical members of the category "predators" are lions and tigers, and humans are nonprototypical members (see Rosch 1975, 1981). This deliberate inclusion of nonprototypical members (humans) in general statements about prototypical ones (lions) hides important differences between the situation of the lion hunting its prey (which no one would argue is unethical) and intensive farming of thousands of animals in cramped conditions. Differences, such as the fact that lions benefit the gene pool of their prey whereas selective breeding for meat quantity damages it, are conveniently hidden.

Potter's (1996: 112–15) investigation of fact construction shows how claims to scientific objectivity are used to "work up the facticity of a version." This can be seen in Ott's case, where his own claims are presented as "biological principles," "biological rules," and "scientific knowledge" based on "biological evidence" (1023–25), while the claims of the animal rights movement are labeled as "beliefs," "fantasies," "philosophical musings," "dogma," "the wrong view," and "false" (1023–29). Hedges such as "might be," "probably," or "can be seen as" are almost never used in Ott's article. Instead the modality throughout the chapter is one that presents what is being talked about as, to use Potter's (1996: 112) words, "solid, unproblematic, and quite separate from the speaker."

While the discourse of evolutionary biology presents animal oppression as "natural" and "inevitable," other discourses use different semantic classifications to make it appear "benign":

> Modern animal housing is well ventilated, warm, well-lit, clean and scientifically designed. . . . Housing protects animals from predators, disease and bad weather. (Animal Industry Foundation quoted in Harnack 1996: 130)

Here the semantic extension of *predators* does not include human predators, such as the farmer, that the housing offers no protection from. This "ontological gerrymandering" (Potter 1996: 186) makes wild animals seem to be the enemy of domesticated ones, with humans their benevolent protectors. As Garner (1998: 463) points out "Agribusiness interests often disguise the grim realities of factory farming and proclaim their concern for animal welfare." This can be seen in the language used in the quotation above. The euphemism "housing" is used in place of "cage," and the five positive qualities of the "housing" are expressed directly one after another other in a list, a grammatical pattern used by real estate agents describing a desirable residence. In a list such as this it is easy to sneak in something dubious among the positives without it being noticed. In this case "scientifically designed" sounds superficially positive, but the housing is scientifically designed for the profit of the farmer, not for the comfort of the animals, who would be much happier with a nonscientifically designed natural habitat.

Like many of the properties described by real estate agents, there are alternative, less euphemistic ways of describing the same accommodation. For example, compare "Modern animal housing is . . . well-lit" with "Crammed into tiny cages with artificial lighting" (Trans-Species Unlimited, quoted in Harnack 1996: 136), and compare "well ventilated, warm . . . clean" with what the poultry industry itself describes as "the heat mixed with the ammonia and dust in the houses causes incredible health problems" (*Poultry* magazine 1997a).

Even punctuation is used for ideological ends, as the example from a dairy industry journal below shows:

> People concerned about animal welfare . . . may have seen a sensational news story about the abuse of animals or about "factory farms." (*Hoard's Dairyman* 1995: 449)

Here the use of quotation marks is intended to try to distance intensive farming from the image of a factory.

While the "external" discourse of animal industries presents the treatment of animals as benign, "internal" discourse has a different ideological objective. Here the aim seems to be to encourage those who work in the industry to neglect suffering and focus on profit. Fiddes (1991: 200) describes the way that the meat industry "regards care for their animal raw materials as little more than a commercial oncost." An indication of this can be found in the archives of the industry magazines *Poultry* and *Meat Marketing and Technology* (www.meatingplace.com). Within these archives at the time they were examined, items in the lexical set "pain, suffering, hurt(ing)" (with reference to animals) were mentioned in 3, 2, and no articles respectively. On the other hand, items in the lexical set "money, financial, profit" were mentioned in 224, 101, and 90 articles respectively.

Hidden assumptions that make the suffering of animals appear unimportant can be found in the linguistic devices used in the discourse of the meat industries. One of these devices is metonymy, which is, according to Lakoff (1987: 77), "one of the basic characteristics of cognition." Examples are as follows (emphasis added):

(a) Catching *broilers* is a backbreaking, dirty and unpleasant job. (*Poultry* magazine 1997a)

(b) [There is] susceptibility to ascites and flipover . . . in the female *breeder* (*Poultry* magazine 1995)

(c) There's not enough power to stun the *beef* . . . you'd end up cutting its head off while the *beef* was still alive. (Slaughterhouse worker interviewed in Eisnitz 1997: 216)

(d) Exciting times for *beef* practitioners (Herrick 1995: 1031)

In (a) live birds are named and referred to by a cooking method, in (b) by their function, in (c) cows are referred to by their dead flesh, and in (d) veterinarians specializing in bovine medicine are called "beef practitioners" rather than "cow practitioners." All of these ways of referring to animals focus attention away from their individuality and contribute to what Regan (1996: 35) calls "the system that allows us to view animals as *our resources.*"

The discourse of resources is frequently used in direct reference to live animals as well as dead ones. Examples are the word *damage* instead of *injury* in the expression "bird *damage*" (*Poultry* magazine 1997b), *product* instead of *bodies* in "*product* is 100 percent cut-up and hand deboned" (*Poultry* magazine 1997b), and *destruction* and *batch* in "Isolation of salmonella will result in the *destruction* of the flock . . . [or] slaughter of the *batch*" (*Poultry* magazine 1995). The discourse of resources includes metaphors too, from dead metaphors such as "live*stock*" to novel metaphors such as the animals-as-plants metaphor evident in "an automatic broiler *harvesting* machine" (*Poultry* magazine 1997a) and "How hogs are handled before stunning and *harvesting* has plenty to do with the quality of meat" (*Meat Marketing & Technology* 1995) (emphasis added in each quotation).

Since inanimate resources cannot suffer, the discursive constriction of animals as resources contributes to an ideology that disregards suffering. When events that include suffering *are* described and talked about, nominalization is frequently used to hide agency (see Fairclough 1989: 124). An example of this is:

Catcher fatigue, absenteeism and turnover can effect broken bones and bruises that reduce processing yields. (*Poultry* magazine 1997a)

This sentence describes incidents where animals are injured. But the actual animals are not mentioned at all. This is accomplished through the nominalizations *broken bones* (X breaks Y's bones) and *bruises* (X bruises Y), which allow the patient, Y, to be deleted. The agent, X, in this case the "catcher," is also deleted, appearing only indirectly as a modifier in the noun phrase "catcher fatigue." And the "catcher fatigue" forms part of the agent of the verb "effect" rather than "break." This distances deliberate human action from animal injuries. In addition, the results of the injuries are not mentioned in terms of pain or suffering, but only in terms of "yields." The same pattern can be seen in this sentence:

> Carcass damage from handling and bird struggle during the kill does occur in broilers (*Poultry* magazine 1997b).

There are three nominalizations here: "damage" (X damages Y), "handling" (X handles Y), and "the kill" (X kills Y). These three hide both the agent and the patient, who appears only as a modifier in the expressions "bird damage" and "bird struggle." In addition, the resultant injuries to what are clearly live, struggling animals are expressed in terms of damage to the dead "carcass."

Singer (1990/1975: 50) points out that "detachment is made easier by the use of technical jargon that disguises the real nature of what is going on." This can be seen in the following quote:

> Perdigo's Marau plant processes 4.95-pound broilers at line speeds of 136 bpm, running 16 hours per day. . . . Perdigo previously used a stunning method more similar to US standards: 45 mA/bird (60 Hz) for a seven second duration with water bath. However, these stunning parameters induced pectoral muscle contraction that resulted in blood splash. (*Poultry* magazine 1997b)

Here birds become units in the mathematically expressed parameters "136 bpm" (birds per minute) and "45 mA/bird." And it is these "stunning parameters" that are the agent of the verb "induced." Thus, responsibility for causing convulsions so strong they cause bleeding is being placed on parameters rather than on the electrocution itself, or the people instigating it.

One final linguistic device that is used to encourage the disregard of animal suffering is extended metaphor, which, as Johnson (1983) shows, can influence reasoning patterns. The following is a famous example of a meat industry metaphor:

> The breeding sow should be thought of as, and treated as, a valuable piece of machinery whose function is to pump out baby pigs like a sausage machine (Walls Meat Company, in Coats 1989: 32)

Regarding pigs as machines encourages metaphorical reasoning along the lines of:

> "machines do not have feelings," so
> "pigs do not have feelings," and
> "valuable machines should be utilized as much as possible," thus
> "pigs should be utilized as much as possible."

The results of this reasoning pattern can be seen in Coats's (1989: 34) description of pig farming: "the sow must produce the maximum number of live piglets in the shortest time. . . . No regard is paid for the distress and suffering caused by these continual pregnancies."

This chapter analyzed a number of materials using the methods of critical discourse analysis in an investigation of the connection between language, power and the oppression of animals. The ultimate aim of analyses such as this is, of course, not simply to describe relations of domination and exploitation, but also to challenge them. Fairclough's (1992b) *Discourse and Social Change* describes the way that dominant ideologies that reproduce and maintain oppression can be resisted, and social change can come about through opposing discourses.

The animal rights movement, as it exists today, does provide a discourse that opposes oppression. Animal rights authors frequently counter the classifications of general discourse by using terms such as "nonhuman animal," "other-than-human animal," and inclusive terms such as "being" in "If a being suffers there can be no moral justification for refusing to take that suffering into consideration" (Singer 1990/1975: 8). This is the same "humans are animals" semantic classification used in biological discourse to argue against animal rights. However, in this case the similarities drawn out are different, focusing on animals' ability to suffer and feel pain in the same way that humans can, rather than predatory aspects.

The animal rights movement is aware of the power of language, and makes deliberate attempts to change language, as the following examples show:

> We chose [pets] and most likely bought them in a manner similar to the way in which human slaves were once . . . bought and sold. . . . Keeping the term pets recognises this hierarchy of ownership. (Belk 1996)

> · The blade is electrically heated and cauterises the blood vessels as it snips off about one fourth of the beak. The chicken industry characterises this procedure as "beak trimming" as if it's *little more than a manicure.* (Marcus 1998: 103, emphasis in original)

> [When animals are considered to be "tools"] a certain callousness towards them becomes apparent. Consider, for instance, Harlow and Suomi's mention of their "rape rack" and the jocular tone in which they report on the "favourite tricks" of the female monkeys. (Singer 1990/1975: 50)

> [About the term "road kill"] I do not believe that humans . . . should refer to innocent, defenceless victims . . . in such an insensitive, impersonal way. . . . I believe that the term "road-kill" should be stricken from our vocabulary. (Appel 2000: 8)

However, these are all focused on individual words. This chapter has attempted to show that it is not just individual words that contribute to the domination and oppression of animals. Instead clusters of language features at all levels, from the morphological changes that create the metonymy "broiler" from "broil," through punctuation, semantic classification schemes, grammatical choices, and pronoun usage, to metaphor are systematically related to underlying ideologies that contribute to maintaining and reproducing oppression.

The external discourses of animal product industries contain hidden ideological assumptions that make animal oppression seem "inevitable, natural, and benign." The internal discourses encourage pain and suffering to be disregarded for the sake of profit. It is not, therefore, just at the level of words that animal activists can attempt to oppose discourses of oppression, but at the level of discourse.

Van Dijk (1993: 253) describes the way that critical discourse analysts take the perspective of "those who suffer most from dominance and inequality. . . . Their problems are . . . serious problems that affect the wellbeing and lives of many." In terms of the sheer number of sentient beings suffering, and the impact that intensive farming has on their lives from birth to slaughter, nonhuman animals fit into this group. This chapter has attempted to show that language is relevant to the oppression of animals, and can be an appropriate area of research for critical discourse analysis. Chapter 2 applies discourse analysis in greater detail, focusing on the one particular animal.

2

As Charming as a Pig

In Victorian Britain, the relationship between people and pigs could be described as one of closeness. Pigs were an integral part of village life, living in close proximity with their owners and being fed on leftover food from the kitchen or even the table (Malcolmson and Mastoris 1998). However, Leach (1964: 51) describes how because pigs were "nearly a member of the household," people felt "a rather special guilt." Leach continues: "After all, sheep provide wool, cows produce milk, chickens produce eggs, but we rear pigs for the sole purpose of killing and eating them, and this is rather a shameful thing, a shame which quickly attaches to the pig itself." This shame manifested itself as an array of insulting expressions related to pigs that entered the English language.

Now the relationship between pigs and humans is one of distance, as the relentless push for cheap pork has led to pigs being kept indoors in intensive conditions. With the aid of technology and machinery a few people look after hundreds of pigs, while for most people the only direct contact they have with pigs is on their dinner plate. However, the intense negativity toward pigs within the English language remains, and since language is intimately bound up with culture, the image of the pig continues to play a part in English culture.

As Fairclough (2003a: 18) points out "cultures exist as languages, or what I shall rather call discourses." The first section of this chapter presents an analysis of how pigs are referred to in general discourse in the UK, followed by a detailed analysis of the discourse of the pork industry in the second section. The final section discusses attempts that have been made to challenge and transcend both general and industry discourse.

GENERAL DISCOURSE

Examining the uses of the word *pig* in a corpus of contemporary English such as the British National Corpus (BNC) reveals just how widespread and negative the constructions of pigs are. The BNC consists of 100 million words extracted from a wide range of books, newspapers, television programs, magazines, and recorded everyday speech. And within the BNC is an astonishingly large range of metaphors, similes, and idioms about pigs, far more than for any other animal. Rats, snakes, dogs, and cats do not even come close, showing how deeply the pig is entrenched in British culture. In total there are sixty-two different nonliteral uses of the words *pig*, *hog*, and *swine* in the corpus, and these are summarized in table 2.1 (a–c).

Even a cursory glance at table 2.1 reveals the overwhelmingly negative attitude toward pigs expressed in everyday British English. With only a few exceptions, such as *you lucky pig* and *happy as a pig in the mire*, the expressions seem to be attributions of unpleasant or negative characteristics to a third (human) party. Examination of the context in which such expressions occur reveals *presuppositions*, taken-for-granted facts about the world that lie behind the expressions (Kadmon 2000, Gazdar 1978). The expression "as fat as a pig" presupposes and takes it to be common knowledge that pigs are (very) fat animals. Extracting and analyzing presuppositions is an effective way of revealing the cultural model, or in Barthes's (1972) terms, the *mythology*, underlying linguistic usage.

Presuppositions are a particularly powerful way of building and sustaining the models on which a culture is based. The expression "as selfish as a pig" presupposes that pigs are (very) selfish, without any kind of overt statement, such as "pigs are selfish," which could be proved wrong. As expressions are repeated in the general currency of society, the mythology of pigs as selfish creatures is perpetuated. An expression such as "foreign pig," of course, does not presuppose that pigs are foreign, and grammatically all sentences of the form "adjective + pig" do not necessarily contain presuppositions. The grammar of the sentence in which the word *pig* is found is therefore important to take into consideration when analyzing presuppositions (hence the arrangement of table 2.1 according to grammatical structures).

TABLE 2.1

A

Grammatical Patterning of *Pig* and Associated Expressions without Presuppositions in BNC

EXPRESSION	GRAMMAR
absolute pig	Adj + N
awful pig	Adj + N
beastly pig	Adj + N
capitalist pig	Adj + N
drunken swine	Adj + N
fascist pigs	Adj + N
fat pig	Adj + N
filthy pig	Adj + N
foreign pigs	Adj + N
greedy pig	Adj + N
ignorant pig	Adj + N
insufferable pig	Adj + N
irritating pig	Adj + N
lucky pig	Adj + N
lying pig	Adj + N
male chauvinist pig	Adj + N
misogynist swine	Adj + N
murderous pigs	Adj + N
patronizing pig	Adj + N
pompous pig	Adj + N
rotten mean pig	Adj + N
savage pig	Adj + N
self-righteous pig	Adj + N
selfish little swine	Adj + N
selfish pig	Adj + N
self-regarding swine	Adj + N
stupid pig	Adj + N
unbelieving swine	Adj + N
unfeeling pig	Adj + N
ungallant swine	Adj + N
unscrupulous swine	Adj + N
untidy pig	Adj + N
old fat pig	Adj + N

TABLE 2.1 (CONTINUED)

B

Grammatical Patterning of *Pig* and Associated Expressions with Meaning-Dependent Presuppositions in BNC

EXPRESSION	GRAMMAR
a pig sty	N (modifier) + N
go the whole hog	Idiom
make a pig's ear of it	Idiom
make a pig's breakfast of it	Idiom
a major pig out	Idiom
to pig out	V + out
she was a pig to me	N
the car's a pig	N
you pig!	N
pig!	N
he is a pig	N
making a pig of herself	N of ref. pronoun
hog the limelight	V

C

Grammatical Patterning of *Pig* and Associated Expressions with Direct Presuppositions in BNC

EXPRESSION	GRAMMAR
as sick as a pig	N (simile)
tuck in like a pig	N (simile)
bleeding like a stuck pig	N (simile)
as fat as a pig	N (simile)
drunk as a pig	N (simile)
happy as a pig in poop	N (simile)
happy as a pig in the mire	N (simile)
rich as a pig in shit	N (simile)
squealing like a stuck pig	N (simile)
sweating like a pig	N (simile)
stubborn as a pig	N (simile)
stinking pig greedy	N (modifier) + Adj
pig sick of them	N (modifier) + Adj
pig ignorant	N (modifier) + Adj

Within the "adjective + pig" category (in table 2.1a) are a range of expressions where "pig" refers to a "person who is improperly assuming superiority": *male chauvinist pig, patronizing pig, misogynist swine, pompous pig, self-righteous pig, self-regarding swine,* and *fascist pig.* However, it would be a mistake to suppose that "assuming superiority" belongs to the cultural model of pigs, since it is not presupposed, and there is no additional evidence of expressions that contain corresponding presuppositions (such as "as patronizing as a pig" or "as misogynist as a pig").

In the expressions in table 2.1b, the presupposition is not explicitly given within the sentence but is, instead, a function of the meaning of the sentence. For example, if "She is behaving like a pig!" is used to mean "She is behaving greedily," then this presupposes that "pigs are greedy." Since the word *greedy* is not explicitly mentioned, it is the readers/hearers of the sentence themselves who must supply the concept of greed. This is what Fairclough (1989: 85) calls "gap-filling," and it is a particularly powerful way of entrenching cultural models since hearers/readers are forced to supply negative presuppositions to interpret the sentences.

Analyzing only direct presuppositions (table 2.1c), and those meaning-dependent presuppositions (table 2.1b) where the context makes the meaning explicit, we can gain an impression of the cultural model behind the use of the word *pig* in the BNC. Of course the BNC itself contains only a fraction of the many uses of the word *pig* in English, but we can get a general idea of just how negative these uses are by using the BNC as a spotlight. According to the data in the BNC, within British culture, pigs are presupposed to be ignorant, greedy, untidy, stubborn, selfish, badly behaved, and fat; to get very drunk and sick; to squeal loudly when "stuck"; to become happy in the "poop" or "shit"; and to have a sloppy breakfast.

While the cultural model bears little relation to actual pigs, it bears all the hallmarks of cultural models in other areas, such as racism or sexism. Members of the dominant group base their feelings of superiority and self-worth on the supposed shortcomings of another group, "basking in the reflection of a negatively constituted other" (Valentine 1998: 2.2).

However, this is a very unstable base for self-esteem, since deep down everyone knows that the other group does not, in fact, have these shortcomings. Rather than finding a new basis for self-esteem, for example cooperation and respect, the supposed shortcomings are simply trumpeted more loudly and entrenched ever deeper in everyday language.

In Victorian times, the inferior image of pigs presumably helped provide a barrier between humans and pigs, overcoming cultural taboos against killing those who are close to us. The discourse of the pork industry could equally be argued to provide a barrier between humans and pigs, although in this case the discourse is very different since it has to justify not just killing pigs, but also keeping them confined indoors in high-intensity facilities during their lifetime.

PORK INDUSTRY DISCOURSE

The discourse of the pork industry can be characterized as scientific and technical. There are therefore no explicit insults: pigs are never officially described as ignorant, selfish, greedy, nasty, or filthy. Yet it is possible, within scientific and technical discourse, to insert hidden ideological assumptions that nonetheless construct pigs in a negative way. It is easy to notice the explicit insults hurled at pigs in general discourse and counter them with facts about, for example, the cleanliness and sociability of pigs. However, noticing the implicit ideological assumptions in technical discourse requires deeper analysis.

This section conducts such an analysis, using the framework of critical discourse analysis (Fairclough 2003a, van Dijk 1993). The analysis focuses on the standard reference manual of the pork industry, the *Pork Industry Handbook* (PIH), a document that both reflects and propagates pork industry discourse. According to its own publicity, the *Pork Industry Handbook* is written by "more than 800 authors and reviewers," and is used in "45 states representing about 99 percent of the pork production in the US" (PIH 2003: 233). And within the information sheets that make up the PIH, hidden among countless instructions for the proper raising of pigs, is nothing less than the redefinition of an entire species.

The PIH states that "Since the early 1970s, the swine industry has continued to move towards specialisation, mechanisation and enclosed housing for the rearing of livestock" (PIH 2002: 104). A similar statement could be made about the language of the PIH, which has become specialized and technologized (to use Fairclough's [1992b] term) to serve the goals of the industry. And the goals are clear: "the business of producing pork is the primary, and most frequently, the only objective" (PIH 2002: 83), "The goal of the workplace is to minimise the amount of time (labor) spent on . . . each animal unit" (PIH 2002: 8), and above all else, "The success of a swine enterprise is measured in terms of profit" (PIH 2002: 100).

To achieve these goals pigs have been linguistically reconceptualized on a fundamental level, starting with a redefinition of the concept of their "health":

> Health is the condition of an animal with regard to the performance of its vital functions. The vital functions of the pig are reproduction and growth. They are vital because they are major contributors to the economic sustainability of the pork production enterprise. (PIH 2002: 140)

Usually, "vital functions" refer to those bodily functions that life depends on, such as digestion or the circulation of blood. However, in the *Pork Industry Handbook* definition above, the bodily functions of the pigs are not vital to the individual animal but to the "pork production enterprise." This metaphorically constructs the enterprise as a huge animate being whose life depends on making a profit, with pigs rendered collectively vital but individually dispensable cells making up this larger being.

Disease is defined in similar terms: "Disease is a major risk to farm sustainability, thus protection of herd health is a top priority" (PIH 2002: 140). Note that the word "health" has been replaced by the term "herd health," helping to create a situation where "verbally subsumed into the flock or herd, nonhumans disappear as individuals" (Dunayer 2001: 140). The PIH (2002: 140) describes the way that designing health strategies "for herds of animals requires a very different approach than those used for individual animals." And when pigs disappear as individuals, their individual health problems also disappear from official consideration.

Individual pigs each have a function in keeping the "enterprise-being" alive, and their lives are defined narrowly in terms of this function. Linguistically, premodifiers are used to incorporate the function into the designation of individuals. Thus we find "nursery pig," "grower pig," "farrowing pig," and "finisher pig" (PIH 2002: 146), as well as "feeder pig" and "market hog" (6), "carry-over sow" (83), "cull sow" (123), and "slaughter hog" (12).

Health is measured solely in terms of ability to perform the desired function, allowing genuine health problems that do not conflict with the function to be ignored. The following are examples extracted from the PIH that illustrate this:

- Pigs can be subjected to very high levels of ammonia for a relatively long time with little adverse production effect (PIH 2002: 54)
- Pigs develop high fevers [from swine flu] . . . exhibit rapid forced breathing . . . a harsh barking cough . . . [and] pregnant animals frequently abort. Although pigs *appear* to be quite ill . . . death loss is minimal (PIH 2002: 141, emphasis added)
- Claw injuries have been shown to be greater on total slats than on partial slats. However, the effect of claw injuries on growth rate appears to be slight (PIH 2002: 53)

In the first quote the irritation and respiratory problems associated with ammonia are ignored because they do not affect the "growth rate." In the second quote, despite the long list of symptoms, pigs only "appear" to be ill, because financial loss due to their death is minimal. In the third quote, injuries to pigs' legs are summarily dismissed because they have little influence on their growth rate. According to the PIH definition of health, pigs are only "actually" ill when their health problems have a financial impact.

Having defined health in terms of the "performance of [the pig's] vital functions" (PIH 2002: 140), the term "health" is often dropped completely and subsumed within the replacement term "performance." This can lead to macabre conclusions, for example, that even if up to a quarter of piglets die due to disease or injury the herd still performs well and hence is "healthy." This can be seen in the quote below, which describes the advantages and disadvantages of removing piglets from their mother early and giving them broad-spectrum antibiotics.

> Postweaning mortality is increased (ranging up to 12% to 25%). . . .
> However, substantial benefits have been reported in the finishing per-
> formance (PIH 2002: 111)

Medical intervention for the sake of "performance" is quite different from medical intervention to save lives or reduce pain. For example, the "hysterectomy-derived, colostrum deprived germ free (microbe free) pigs" (PIH 2002: 139) are produced by "opening the uterus and extracting the pigs by hysterectomy" and then rearing them "in isolation . . . on artificial milk replacer" (PIH 2002: 139). The result: "infections disease levels may be low and pig performance excellent" (PIH 2002: 139).

Fortunately for the pigs, since shivering wastes "feed energy to frictional losses that would otherwise go to growth" (PIH 2002: 54), the PIH recommends keeping them warm, although it expresses this as "optimal thermal conditions for pork production" (54). However, not all measures that improve productivity are so comfortable for the pigs. In particular "the amount of space needed per pig for optimal performance" (PIH 2002: 55) does not correspond to the amount of space a pig needs to move comfortably, as becomes clear in the following quote:

> Cages for weaned pigs have zestfully captured the attention of pork
> producers. They do offer . . . improved pig performance. A 4 × 4 ft. cage
> will accommodate a litter of about 8 pigs up to 40lb. (PIH 2002: 70)

However, the comfort and well-being of pigs *is* mentioned in several places in the PIH. For example: PIH (2002: 69) recommends planning for "*animal com-fort* . . . and labor efficiency"; PIH (2002: 140) describes the effect of disease on "performance . . . and *animal well-being*"; and PIH (2002: 146) recommends "euthanasia" as the best option for "various *pig welfare* reasons" as well as "eco-nomic" reasons (emphasis added). The pattern is clear: The word "pig" is used as a modifier of the words "comfort," "well-being," or "welfare," making expressions like "pig comfort" appear to be a variable in equations. And frequently, in proximity to "pig comfort" are expressions relating to economic factors. For example, "while dry bedding can be used to keep pigs more comfortable, it is expensive . . . and is not compatible with . . . slotted floors" (PIH 2002: 66). However, "pig welfare" is not quantifiable and so drops out of the mathematical equations that ultimately determine the conditions that pigs must endure. For example, the following equation defines mortality:

$$\text{Percent mortality} = \frac{\text{No. died in nursery and/or growing-finishing stage}}{\text{Total no. entering for this group}} \times 100$$

(PIH 2002: 100)

Mortality is a variable that is optimized for maximum profit. One of the tables provided by the PIH (2002: 100, table 2.1) suggests that in a farm with "excellent performance," mortality is less than 10 percent from birth to weaning, the amount of space pigs live in is less than 2.8 square feet, and more than 2,500 hogs are produced per full-time laborer per year. The tables and jargon and equations hide an ideology that seems to dictate, in the pursuit of profit, that pigs should be as crowded and neglected as possible, but not so much so that a financially significant percentage die.

The death of pigs due to the diseases and injuries associated with intensive farming is rendered not as a tragedy, but as a purely economic consideration through the phrase "death loss" in the following quote:

In large continuous flow operations . . . death loss and the number of chronically ill poor-doing pigs that result may be quite high. (PIH 2002: 141)

The use of the expression "death loss" avoids mentioning who died, and is used elsewhere as a euphemism for the "dead bodies of pigs" who die from illness or injury: "In a typical scenario, a bin is filled with three months death losses" (133).

Among the "death losses" are animals who, having been ill, injured, or unprofitably small in size have been the subject of another euphemism, what PIH

(2002: 146) calls "humane euthanasia" (see Dunayer 2001: 137, 141). The fact that this is a euphemism is illustrated by the description of one method for performing "humane euthanasia," which instructs the farmer to "hold the piglet by its hind legs and forcefully hit the piglet's head against a hard surface such as concrete" (PIH 2002: 18). The use of the pronoun "it" in this quote is perhaps not accidental, since it makes the piglet seem more like an object than a baby, making it easier to kill her. The pronouns "he" and "she" are, in fact, used in the PIH for less violent scenarios, but pigs are often referred to by the pronoun "it" (e.g., in PIH 2002: 54, 140, 58, 122, 128, 87).

Another way that pigs are objectified is through the use of the metaphor "pig as a machine" (Coats 1989: 32). Singer (1990/1975: 126) quotes the pork industry's explicit statement that a sow should be "thought of, and treated as, a valuable piece of machinery." However, the PIH itself contains no such direct linking of pigs to machines, perhaps because animal rights activists use such examples to illustrate the cruelty of the pork industry. Instead, the PIH uses expressions that *presuppose* that pigs are machines, making the ideology both covert and more powerful. The following quotes are examples of this, with emphasis added:

- As long as boars remain *structurally sound* and are aggressive breeders, fertility is generally maintained. (PIH 2002: 1)
- Adequate *boar power* is critically essential to take advantage of synchronization of postweaning heat. (PIH 2002: 8)
- Pigs suppress eating and increase *water intake* during periods of heat stress. (PIH 2002: 54)
- To prevent *sow breakdown* make sure the lactation ration is properly fortified. (PIH 2002: 8)
- *Sow durability* and temperament are very important considerations. (PIH 2002: 145)

There are many other examples from the PIH where pigs are represented metaphorically as inanimate objects. Pigs are described in terms of resources that are "produced" (PIH 2002: 85) and have "salvage value" (PIH 2002: 8). They appear in lists with other kinds of resources, for example, "efficient flow of feed, hogs and waste" (PIH 2002: 70). The word "damage" is used rather than "injury" (PIH 2002: 8); piglets are "processed" (tails cut off, teeth cut, ears cut, castrated) (PIH 2002: 18); boars are "used" (PIH 2002: 83) and sows are talked about in terms of "volume slaughtered" rather than number slaughtered (PIH 2002: 132).

In another form of objectification, there are cases in the PIH where the distinction between living animals and meat products becomes blurred. Hedgepeth (1998: 76) describes this as a difficulty in viewing "hogs as hogs rather than as neatly packaged collected assortments of ambulatory pork." Adams (1993: 204) captures the attitude with the simple expression "To be a pig is to be pork." The following quotes are examples of this confusion between living animals and meat:

- Some hogs have weak hindquarters, and they are more likely to fall down and "split." The damaged meat has to be trimmed. (PIH 2002: 116)
- Choosing a meaty, lean herd sire will probably do more to improve carcass leanness than will altering various environmental aspects. (PIH 2002: 100)
- One should incorporate meat-type animals into the breeding herd. (PIH 2002: 26)

The creation of a high-intensity pig farm demands a great deal of technology, including cages, farrowing stalls, and machines to regulate the environment and flow of feed and waste. But as important as the technology is language itself, because language plays a central role in the design, construction, and everyday operation of the farm. When pigs are represented as objects or machines, and their health and lives are defined narrowly in terms of profitability, then this both justifies and provides a blueprint for a system of farming that is both inhumane and environmentally destructive. Nowhere does the discourse of the PIH explicitly state that pigs should be treated as objects, that their pain and misery should be ignored, that they are just pork rather than animals. Instead, the ideology is covertly conveyed and perpetuated in the equations, tables, technical jargon and in the presuppositions that permeate the handbook. And the ideology is all the more powerful and resistant to criticism through being covert.

ALTERNATIVE DISCOURSES

When ideology is implicit, it cannot be resisted through direct opposition of the propositional content of the language it is embedded in, since the ideology appears only indirectly in presuppositions. For example, texts rarely explicitly say that animals are worthless beings who can be treated however humans wish, but instead convey that message implicitly through the words chosen to represent animals. However, ideology *can* be challenged through analysis that exposes the models that underlie discourses and the interests that they serve. Critical language awareness has, in fact, been a part of the animal rights movement since its inception. Singer (1990/1975) describes the appalling conditions on pig farms and intersperses his description with quotations from pork industry sources, revealing the relationship between industry discourse and the conditions in which pigs are forced to live and die. Dunayer (2001) goes further by explicitly describing the relationship between language and oppression and conducting linguistic analysis of a variety of discourses that construct pigs and other animals. Such critical language awareness has the potential to undermine discourses by revealing their hidden ideological assumptions, and thus taking away the power that implicitness gives them (see Fairclough 1992a, 1999).

In addition to raising critical language awareness, Dunayer (2001: 179–201) provides a complete set of guidelines for "countering speciesism," which could be considered a form of *verbal hygiene* (Cameron 1995). For "bacon, ham, pork (etc.)" the guidelines recommend "pig flesh" (Dunayer 2001: 193). An alternative for "pork producer" is "pig enslaver" (194), "cull" is "murder" (194), a "farm" is a "confinement facility," and the farmer is a "nonhuman-animal exploiter" (195).

Overt attempts to change discourses, however, run into an effective weapon used by conservative society to resist social change: the charge of "political correctness." Frequently, the media create absurd examples that mock any attempt to change language. Mills (2003: 89) gives the examples of "vertically challenged" and "personhole cover." Non-speciesist language guidelines are receiving similar treatment. Lists of pseudo "politically correct" terms related to animals have started appearing on a number of humorous websites: examples are "hen rapery" for battery egg farm, "seared mutilated animal flesh" for hamburgers, "stolen nonhuman animal fibres" for wool, and even "quadruped nonhuman associate" for feline companion (i.e., cat).

A way of providing alternative discourses that avoids the issue of "correctness" is *poetic activism*. Poetic activism is based on the appreciation of "the power of language to make new and different things possible and important — an appreciation which becomes possible only when one's aim becomes an expanding repertoire of alternative descriptions rather than The One Right Description" (Rorty, in Gergen 1999: 63). While verbal hygiene tends to represent its prescriptive alternatives as more accurate, truthful, or "correct," poetic activism offers "provocative, glamouring, and compelling ways of talking and writing, ways that unsettle the common sense, taken for granted realities, and invite others into new dialogic spaces" (Gergen 2000).

A good example of poetic activism applied to pigs is Hedgepeth's (1998) *The Hog Book*. Hedgepeth first challenges dominant discourses through parody and irony (rather than claims of falsehood), and then supplies new ways of thinking about pigs through the application of new discursive constructions:

> "Hog," to many people means any obscenely rotund beast with a tropism for mud who trundles filthily along oinking." (Hedgepeth 1998: 21)

In the above quote, Hedgepeth uses parody to challenge general discourse about pigs by exaggerating it and making it appear absurd. He does the same for industry discourses in the following quote:

> [In an artificial insemination system] sows are viewed as simple pork machines and boars are vaguely undesirable characters who happen to

make sperm. . . . [The system has] the aim of turning out germ-free, computer-recorded pieces of living pigmeat. (99)

Hedgepeth's reconstruction of pigs employs novel metaphors, such as the "human body as pig grave" metaphor with which the book commences:

> DEDICATED . . . to the millions of porkers who've gone to their final resting sites inside us. . . . I'd like to call them all by name, but the list is long and I cannot remember. (Hedgepeth 1998)

This metaphor resists the industry's "To be a pig is to be pork" ideology by providing an unusual way of emphasizing the individuality of pigs. Throughout the book, there are countless explicit statements and presuppositions that reconstruct pigs as "clear-headed, perspicacious beings with feelings" (160).

To provide a "new definition of hogness," Hedgepeth uses intertextual borrowing (Fairclough 1992b: 101) to apply discourses from other domains to the human-pig relationship. One of these intertextual borrowings makes use of the discourse of psychology: "Cultural Hogrophobia . . . is a socially institutionalized fear of hogness" (Hedgepeth 1998: 6). Later he claims that

> we rely upon the hog in many ways for support and for a sense of definition—definition of ourselves, for instance, as presumably superior, handsomer and all-round more legitimate creatures. It's in this way that we subconsciously employ the hog. (200)

Drawing on the discourse of self-help psychology, Hedgepeth claims that in coming to terms with hogrophobia you can develop a "new hog consciousness" (197) and "eventually emerge as a changed and better person" (x). This change is constructed not just as psychological growth but spiritual growth too, through intertextual borrowings from the domain of spiritual discourse. The following quotes illustrate the use of spiritual discourse to contribute to what Hedgepeth calls a "massive redefinition of hogness for the new age" (26):

> True "hogritude"—the mystical essence and condition of being an actual hog—demands extended periods of meditation. (173)

> The all-pervasive essence of Hog had resonated across time and in-
> sinuated itself deep into . . . our collective mind. [We are] awaiting some
> hopeful opportunity to transcend ourselves . . . [and pigs provide] . . .
> an ideal agent for inducing us to break our narrow containments . . . and
> thereby scale new heights of enlightenment and psychic liberation. (198)

Like his parodies of the discourses of oppression, Hedgepeth's application of psychological and spiritual discourse to pigs is exaggerated, tongue-in-cheek and not intended to be taken (too) seriously. Through this creative use of language, Hedgepeth resists mainstream discourse and replaces it with an entirely new way of constructing pigs. There is no hint in Hedgepeth's works that this new way is somehow "correct," or the only possible way of reconstructing pigs. *The Hog Book* therefore forces open the door of limited mainstream discourse, takes some bold steps out to create new alternatives, but, crucially, leaves the door wide open to other novel ways of constructing pigs.

In the end, a pig farm is essentially a relationship: a relationship between two groups who happen to be from different species, one human and one porcine. The trend toward the end of the twentieth and the start of the twenty-first century is for this relationship to be increasingly remote, with decisions that have profound consequences on the lives of pigs being taken in distant, air-conditioned offices. And the increasingly citified general population is far more likely to come across pigs in insulting linguistic expressions than face-to-face. The relationship, therefore, becomes more and more mediated by language.

Textual mediation in itself is neither good nor bad. Clearly, discourse has the power to legitimize relationships in which one group causes immense suffering to the other. And the many examples from the pork industry discussed in this chapter suggest that the discourse of the pork industry is doing exactly that. But equally, language can be used imaginatively to resist dominant discourses and open up new alternatives, as Dunayer (2001), Hedgepeth (1998), and others are attempting to do. If these attempts are successful, future generations may refer to pigs as "enslaved nonhumans," or as "creatures of boundless charm and enchantment" (Hedgepeth 1998: 160). Whatever the change is, change is necessary, and Hedgepeth (1998: 199) eloquently expresses the reason why:

> And so we go on about the routine exploitation of our hogs in the name of Agriculture or Industry & Commerce or Better Pork; and in the end it all contributes to the vast-scale devaluation of life itself, for one cannot deny the legitimacy of another creature without diminishing one's own.

3

FROM FLU-LIKE VIRUS TO DEADLY DISEASE

On April 4, 2001, Vandana Shiva wrote in the *Guardian*:

> In Britain, we see the army mobilised to kill a million or more farm animals and bury them in mass graves.

It turned out worse than that. In the end, the 2001 foot-and-mouth epidemic in the UK resulted in the slaughter of at least 6 million animals (4.9 million sheep, 0.7 million cattle, and 0.4 million pigs) — the worst outbreak of foot-and-mouth disease in recorded history (Royal Society 2002). The welfare implications were major, as animals starved in fields because of movement restrictions and some injured animals "survived hours, or even days, after a slaughter operation" (BBC 2001). Foot-and-mouth, however, is not a fatal disease, cannot spread to humans, and a vaccine is available. It is "quite similar to the common cold virus" (Donaldson 2000) and amounts to, in the words of Freedland (2001), a "flu for animals."

What is surprising is that, even though the UK is known as a nation of animal lovers with an active animal rights movement, the killings occurred *without significant protest*. It is the contention of this chapter that the influence of the British media, in the cognitive structuring of the virus in the minds of the population, was the crucial factor justifying what Freedland (2001) calls the "collective madness" of the mass slaughter.

This chapter analyzes metaphors used in a 200,000-word corpus of news reports about the foot-and-mouth crisis gathered from four national British newspapers, the BBC news website, and the *Farmer's Guardian*. These were collected from online archives from mid-February 2001, when the disease first appeared, to the end of May 2001, when the number of new cases started trailing off. (Note: Data from the corpus are referred to by the name, day, and month of the publication. The year of all the data in the corpus is 2001)

Central to how anyone treats animals is their *individual knowledge*. This knowledge is structured in people's minds through various models, such as prototypes (Rosch 1981), scripts (Schank and Abelson 1977), schemata, networks, and metaphors (Lakoff and Johnson 1999). However, individuals do not live in isolation, and the same cognitive structures are often shared among members of groups, leading to *social cognition* (van Dijk 1997, 1993, 1988). The primary way for cognitive structures to be transferred among people is through being embedded in *discourses* — the characteristic ways of using language associated with particular institutions or groups. Discourses are more than just ways of using language — they encode the models that groups use to construct their own version of reality (Fairclough 1989: 16). People are exposed to the models of reality used by specific groups when they come into contact with discourse produced by the group, either through personal interaction or through the media (van Dijk 1988: 108).

Metaphor is one of the most important elements of social cognition. Indeed, according to Lakoff and Johnson (1999: 118), "everyday thought is largely metaphorical." When the metaphors embedded in discourse act *for* the interests of the group that uses that discourse, and *against* the interests of other groups, they could be called *ideological metaphors*.

The two main groups involved in dealing with the foot-and-mouth crisis were the National Farmers Union and the UK government. These two groups consciously or unconsciously structured the concept of foot-and-mouth disease in ways that, arguably, benefited their own interests against the interests of other groups, particularly the animals, but also the tourist industry. The primary interest of the Farmers Union was to keep open foreign markets for British products by attempting to localize the disease and stamp it out as quickly as possible, but without using vaccination, since that would have led to restrictions on exports. The government needed to be seen to act decisively to protect the farmers' interests.

Public representatives of the two groups included the president of the National Farmers Union, the prime minister, the agriculture minister, and government-appointed experts such as the chief vet and chief scientist. These representatives had privileged access to the media, since they were the ones journalists relied on for the quotations and information that made up the news reports (see Fowler 1991). This allowed them to spread the cognitive structures used within their group, including ideological metaphors, to the wider population. The more society at large used the same metaphors in their thinking processes as the government, the less likely they were to oppose the actions that the government was taking.

Within the materials examined, as expected, the majority of direct and indirect quotations and information appearing in the news reports came from representatives of the farmers, the government, and the experts they employed. The speed with which the foot-and-mouth crisis unfolded and the limited number of commentators appearing in the news meant that the construction of reality by these groups was only occasionally challenged. The two main metaphors used by the media for structuring the concept of foot-and-mouth were *war* and *fire*.

What was foot-and-mouth disease? Was it "just like a dose of flu" (*Independent* April 29) or, as one farmer put it, "a powerful enemy . . . [whose] foot soldiers are beyond number and its capacity for harm beyond imagination" (*Independent* March 19)? The vet, Neil Frame, described foot-and-mouth at the time as a "Blitzkrieg of disease ripping through the country," although he went on to complain about how "difficult the disease can be to see in sheep" (*Farmer's Guardian* March 23). Whatever foot-and-mouth was, the primary way it was structured in the media in 2001 was as a war.

The *Telegraph* called the "nerve-centre" of the operation to tackle foot-and-mouth a "bunker," which "has the appearance . . . of a war-room during the worst of the Blitz" (*Telegraph* March 4). From this war room, the ministry launched what the newspaper called "pre-emptive strikes" (*Independent* March 15) against sheep and pigs, killing thousands of healthy animals. The British Army was "mobilised" (*Independent* March 20), led by Brigadier Birtwistle, a game hunter whose "military career is said to have given him the perfect credentials for waging war on the spread of foot-and-mouth disease" (BBC 29 March).

With the army involved and mass killing going on, it was possible that readers/viewers lost sight of the fact that the "war" was a metaphor, a cognitive way of structuring the complex domain of the disease and its economic consequences using the simpler domain of war. The virus was constructed as the enemy, a "formidable," "powerful enemy" (*Independent* March 19), which "attacks cattle, pigs, [and] sheep" (*Telegraph* Feb. 22). However, those who were "in the frontline of the battle" (*Guardian* Feb.25) did not have the virus in their sights. Instead, their targets were the very same cattle, pigs, and sheep who were being "attacked" by the virus.

The disease could, alternatively, have been dealt with non-metaphorically, that is, as a disease, and treated by caring for sick animals (who recover after a few weeks), vaccinating susceptible animals, and letting natural immunity take its course. But, because of the war metaphor, vets took on a new role in the crisis, killing rather than curing animals. One vet was "keen to make a contribution to what resemble[d] a war effort" (*Independent* March 21), while the vice president of the British Veterinary Association was calling for "a professional Territorial Army of vets" (*Farmer's Guardian* May 25).

So why was a war metaphor used? One reason is that war provided a means for the government to appease the farming lobby by placing themselves in the position of ally and focusing attention on a common foe. The agriculture minister at the time, Nick Brown, told farmers in Devon that the government would "fight shoulder to shoulder with them to defeat the epidemic" (*Telegraph* March 27). When relations became strained, he told the farmers, "The war we should be fighting is against the virus. To be fighting each other is a ridiculous thing to do" (*Telegraph* March 16).

The reason farmers, particularly those whose farms were not in immediate danger, supported the war metaphor is that they wanted the disease stopped before it arrived on their farm and caused reduced productivity and inconvenience in terms of looking after sick animals. And they wanted it stopped fast, avoiding vaccination "at all costs" (*Farmer's Guardian* April 20), so that they could sell their meat abroad without restrictions.

War metaphors justified taking drastic military action to achieve these financial goals: "As a military man, [Brigadier Birtwistle] knows the importance of precise planning and *tough action* to achieve what he has described as 'an *apocalyptic* task'" (BBC 29 March, emphasis added). The military, through their involvement alone, embodied and entrenched the war metaphor.

Roger Ward, of the National Farmers Union at the time, directly invoked the war metaphor to justify killing animals on uninfected farms:

> In any war when you're fighting an enemy, and the virus was the enemy, there'll be innocent victims. That's very regrettable and one's heart goes out to those farming families that have had their livestock destroyed. (BBC News 11 May)

Notice that the "innocent victims" here are not the animals but the "farming families." Three days later a BBC news report stated, "Farmers are the obvious victims of the outbreak of foot-and-mouth" (BBC March 14), and in nearly all the other materials examined it was farmers, rather than animals, who were presented as victims.

Franklin (2007) investigates visual images from newspapers at the time, giving examples where sheep were pictured together with farmers, including a photograph of a farmer surrounded by sheep in a field, and a female farmer "depicted in a Madonna-like aspect holding her threatened sheep" (181). The inclusion of the farmer in the picture is compatible with the idea that the farmer is the victim. One photograph in the *Telegraph* (16 March), however, defies the trend and represents the sheep on their own, causing Franklin (2007: 176) to describe the sheep as "a study group of Cheviots whose solidarity and dignity are reinforced by the absence of any humans." The language in the article, however, does not support the image of sheep as dignified victims. Ben

Gill, the president of the National Farmers' Union is reported as saying that the measures taken by the government would leave farmers "desperate and appalled" and create "swathes of dead farmland." By focusing on the impact on the farmers and describing the consequences as "dead farmland" rather than dead or suffering animals, this wording again disguises the role of animals as primary victims.

Lakoff (1991) points out that in the cognitive structuring of a war scenario there are three main participants, "a villain, a victim, and a hero." In the case of foot-and-mouth, the victim is the farmer, the villain is the virus, and the hero is the government. If animals had been placed in the subject position of victims in this scenario, then this would have placed the army in the unjustifiable role of being deployed to kill innocent victims. Instead, animals became the *targets* of the killings, a role usually reserved for the villain. There were a few attempts to portray animals as the agents of the virus, where "suspect sheep" (BBC 16 March) were "harbouring the foot-and-mouth virus" (*Telegraph* March 17), and "spread[ing] the disease" (*Telegraph* March 23), but these attempts were half-hearted. There was no talk of "deadly carriers of the disease" or the like, because it is hard to make a sheep with a mild illness play the role of villain. This left animals with no role within the war metaphor. Instead, the fact that the animals were the ones being killed in this war was hidden through the language used. Instead of "killing animals," a variety of euphemistic metaphors were used. The BBC (May 11) wrote about fields being "cleared," while in the *Times*, animals were "lost" (Feb. 21). In one article in the *Farmer's Guardian*, animals are "taken out," "eliminated," "removed," and even "disappeared" (*Farmer's Guardian* March 23).

The animals were disappearing, certainly, but only from the media discourse surrounding foot-and-mouth. When words like "kill" or "slaughter" were used, the animals themselves were often simply left out, as in "slaughtering out *the infection*" (BBC April 30), "culling *his farm*" (BBC March 29), "kill *out* only where the disease strikes" (*Farmer's Guardian* 6 April) (emphasis added). Even at their own cremation animals were made to disappear when the *Telegraph* (Feb

26) wrote of farmers who saw "their livelihoods thrown on to the bonfires . . . [and] watched the cremation without ceremony of their livelihood" (*Telegraph* Feb. 26).

All of these ways of taking animals out of the picture hid the fact that within the metaphor of war animals were implicitly being made to play the role of enemy soldier. This role is made explicit only in the few voices of opposition to the slaughter policy that reached the press. George Monbiot wrote about "the government's declaration of war with Britain's sheep" (*Guardian* March 29), and Vandana Shiva wrote that "paranoia . . . is moving the military might of Britain to declare a war against its hoofed inhabitants" (*Guardian* April 4).

The second major, and simultaneous, way that the disease was conceptualized was through the metaphor of fire. Foot-and-mouth was, according to the *Times* (February 22), "the forest fire of diseases," which was "raging out of control" (*Independent* March 25). Fires must be stamped out, except that in this case foot-and-mouth had to be "stamped out by slaughter" (*Times* March 28). This justified killing any animals who had the disease.

But in addition to this, the forest fire metaphor also led to, and justified, the killing of healthy animals. In a mixture of metaphors, "Tony Blair . . . stepped up the war against foot-and-mouth ordering [a] precautionary 'firebreak cull'" (*Telegraph* March 23). The following statement from the *Farmer's Guardian* (March 30) shows clearly how the metaphorical "firebreak" leads to the killing of healthy animals: "On the island of Anglesey all sheep in a 50 square mile area are being culled . . . to create a 'firebreak.'"

In the forest fire metaphor, the animals took on the role of trees, with those "animals in the line of spread sacrificed" (*Farmer's Guardian* March 9). It is an unfortunate fact that in a forest fire some trees must be burned as a firebreak in order to save thousands of other trees. However, in the case of a fire, the thousands of other trees would otherwise be consumed and destroyed by fire. In contrast, in the case of foot-and-mouth, animals become ill for a few weeks before recovering. Fighting fire with fire is the metaphor, but in reality this meant fighting a mild animal illness with mass slaughter. In the same way that the presence of the army gave a disturbing concreteness to the metaphor of fighting the virus, the newspaper photographs of piles of burning animal bodies gave a literal edge to the metaphor of forest fire.

The fire metaphor allowed the government, in the form of the agriculture minister, to claim that foot-and-mouth had been "contained" and was "under control" (*Telegraph* March 12) in the run up to an election, although the *Independent* (March 22) asked "In what sense, precisely, is it under control?"

The case study of foot-and-mouth disease presented in this chapter illustrates the workings of ideological metaphor in the media. The model described is one of interested parties in positions of power using the reliance of the press on their quotes and information to spread cognitive structures, including metaphors, that justify their actions. These metaphors contribute to the forming of social cognition, as large numbers of people within the population adopt and use the same structures in their thought and discourse.

In the case of foot-and-mouth, the structuring of the disease by the government and farmers revolved around the ideological metaphors of warfare and fire. These, it is argued, contributed to a way of thinking that resulted in, and was used to justify, the suffering and mass killing of healthy and recuperating animals.

Predominant cognitive structures can be challenged, however, as can be seen in the occasional voices of opposition to the government that appeared in the newspapers. The war metaphor is made to seem absurd when it is pointed out that "the blitz has been equated with 1,500 cattle becoming mildly ill" (*Independent* April 29). What was missing from the news was alternative metaphors for constructing the illness, ones that recognized that the only crime the animals had committed was having blisters in their mouths, not being able to eat for a while, and therefore providing less meat for the farmer, who would eventually kill them anyway.

Foot-and-mouth disease is a mild, non-fatal illness. However, through ideological metaphors dispersed through the media the illness was constructed as a deadly virus that must be fought and stamped out, in all circumstances and at any cost. As this led to the immediate slaughter of any animal who even came close to having the disease, the cognitive structuring itself converts a relatively harmless illness into a truly deadly disease.

4

Counter-Discourses: Animals in Ecology and Environmentalism

When we look back at the extraordinary progress humanity has made during the last 100 years, our satisfaction is inevitably marred by what has happened to the relationship between humans and other animals. While oppression and cruelty toward others may always have existed, the number of animals who have their lives ended or made miserable by human activity is now entirely unprecedented. Each year 10 billion birds and mammals are raised and killed in just one country, the United States, most of them confined "so tightly that they are unable to stretch their limbs or walk even a step or two" (Singer 2003: 3). It seems unlikely that people simply became more cruel as their countries developed; the explanation seems to lie more in the distance of the relationship between an increasingly urban population and animals living out their lives far away behind locked doors.

Donovan (1993: 185) suggests that "we should not kill, eat, torture, and exploit animals because they do not want to be so treated, and we know that. If we listen, we can hear them." Listening, in this sense, necessitates a relationship of observation and empathy that is close enough to understand the fundamental needs of other animals. In the same way that humans have needs for protection, affection, participation, and recreation (Max-Neef 1992), other animals also have needs beyond the minimum for sustaining their lives. Learning to listen again is important not only for relieving the suffering of animals, but also for relieving the psychological damage that is occurring in technological societies as humans become isolated from each other, from other animals, and from nature (see

Clinebell 1996, Roszak, Gomes, and Kanner 1995). In Shepard's (1995: 40) view, "our profound love of animals has been . . . twisted into pets, zoos, decorations, and entertainment," and needs to be refound as part of the process of becoming fully human.

But there is an equally pressing ecological reason why it is important to listen to other animals. In the optimal environment for animals — the natural environment to which they are adapted by their evolution — animals play an integrated role in maintaining balanced ecosystems. As Ekins, Hillman, and Hutchinson (1992: 50) point out, a natural system is "a totally renewable, no-waste economy powered by the sun"; in other words, no inputs other than the sun's energy are required and all waste is used up by other processes. Compare this to the unnatural environments of intensive farms, where animals are deliberately prevented from living according to their nature. These farms suck in (and waste) huge amounts of grain and other foodstuffs, and disgorge environmentally damaging waste. Other ways of going against animals' nature include destroying or fragmenting their habitats, hunting wild animals on an industrial scale, forcing animals to adapt to monoculture environments, and introducing invasive species, all of which can damage the ecosystems on which life depends (see Miller 2002).

As Capra (1997) shows, making human systems as close as possible to natural systems can have beneficial consequences for humans, other animals, and all life. Such systems can only be created by "following the examples in the natural world, rather than always seeking to improve on or second guess them" (Ekins et al. 1992: 50), which entails creating relationships with other animals in which it is possible empathise with and understand, rather than violate, their natures.

Relationships among humans are partially constructed through language. For example, the existence and use of insulting and offensive epithets does not merely reflect relationships of hate; the words themselves are the building blocks of such relationships. The importance of language lies in the way that, as Halliday (2001: 179) describes, "our 'reality' is not something ready-made and waiting to be meant — it has to be actively construed; and . . . language evolved in the process of, and as the agency of, its construal."

The relationship between humans and other animals is, therefore, partially constructed by the language used to talk to and about them. Some people, for instance, patronize and command pets in speech, establishing relationships of domination; and the names of animals are frequently spoken as insults (*dog*, *pig*, *snake*, etc.). There have recently been a number of detailed studies of specialist discourses: those of the animal product industries, pharmaceutical industries, zoos, hunting, and circuses (e.g., Glenn 2004, Dunayer 2001). The studies reveal how, within these discourses, metaphors, grammatical constructions, pronouns, and other linguistic features portray nonhuman animals as objects, machines, or inferior beings, and so contribute to the moral licensing of otherwise unconscionable levels of cruelty to animals.

In opposition to oppressive discourses such as these, influential counter-discourses have arisen, including a great variety related to animal liberation, animal rights, ecology, and the environmental movement. An important question is whether these counter-discourses promote and enable the construction of human-animal relationships in more harmonious ways. For all the reasons suggested above, harmonious relationships can be defined as those in which humans respect other animals, listen to them, accept the validity of their realities, and allow them (as far as possible) to live according to their own natures.

There are, of course, many counter-discourses, and many strands within each. Far from being a complete review, therefore, the following sections focus on aspects of influential counter-discourses that are particularly relevant to constructing relationships between humans and other animals.

THE DISCOURSE OF ECOLOGY AND ECOLOGICAL ECONOMICS

Through the metaphor of "ecosystem," the discourse of ecology represents biological organisms (animals, plants, and micro-organisms) as interdependent and sustained by interactions among themselves and with their physical environment. This opens the way to conceptualize more equitable relationships between humans and other animals, based on mutual dependence, symbiosis, and a nonhierarchical acceptance of all species, including humans, as co-inhabitants of larger ecosystems. In other words, the discourse of ecology could contribute to the "land ethic" proposed by Leopold (1966: 240): "In short, a land ethic changes the role of *Homo sapiens* from conqueror of the land-community to plain member and citizen of it. It implies respect for his fellow-members, and also respect for the community as such."

However, as McNeill (2000: 335) points out, ecologists in the past have tended to pretend that humans did not exist: "Rather than sully their science with the uncertainties of human affairs, they sought out pristine patches in which to monitor energy flows and population dynamics. Consequently they had no political, economic—or ecological—impact." And, we could add, limited impact on improving relationships between human and other animals.

Subsequent approaches to ecology, including *human ecology* and *ecological economics*, have attempted to include humans in the larger picture. However, there is still a reluctance among some strands of human ecology to use discourse that places humans *within* ecosystems. For example, the Ecological Society of America (1997: 4) writes: "Humanity obtains from natural ecosystems an array of ecosystem goods—organisms and their parts and products." This kind of language promotes a conceptualization of ecosystems as existing separately from humans, like supermarkets for humans rather than as systems where all life is mutually sustained. Ecosystems and all the animals within become treated as human resources, as in the following example from an ecology textbook:

> Ecosystems generate ecological resources and services that are crucial for human welfare . . . an ecosystem . . . consists of and sustains a unique array of biotic or "living" components . . . many of which also support human production or consumption . . . we refer to these as *ecological resources* (Barbier, Burgess, and Folke 1994)

This extract metaphorically constructs "ecosystems" as machines for creating human resources, by combining the term "ecosystem" with terms from the discourse of machines ("array" and "components"). Animals, in this case, are "biotic components" of a machine generating resources for human consumption. This kind of discourse seems to have failed to break away from the assumption that animals are resources for humans—the same assumption adopted by exploitative discourses.

Daly and Farley's textbook *Ecological Economics: Principles and Applications* provides a particularly clear example of the portrayal of animals as resources. In one section, Daly and Farley (2004: 34) provide a quotation from the World Wildlife Fund (WWF) which asserts that "the state of Earth's natural ecosystems has declined by about 33 per cent over the last 30 years." They then reexpress this in their own terms: "this means that the capacity of natural capital . . . to supply life support services has declined by about 33%" (Daly and Farley 2004: 34). In reconstruing the WWF statement using the discourse of economics, they fail to heed Ekins et al.'s (1992: 50) warning that "to refer to the Earth, including its wealth of living systems, as 'ecological capital' is already to devalue it."

The problem lies in the extent to which Daly and Farley use the discourse of economics in making their case. Daly and Farley's book is based on the important insight that "the economic system is a subsystem of the global ecosystem" (Daly and Farley 2004: 61). However, the language they to use represent the larger ecosystem is based on terms borrowed from the subsystem—economics. The following are examples of this:

- The structural elements of an ecosystem are stocks of biotic and abiotic resources (minerals, water, trees, other plants and animals), which when combined together generate ecosystem . . . services. (94)
- Intact ecosystems are funds that provide ecosystem services, while their structural components are stocks that provide a flow of raw materials. (104)

This model subsumes the entire natural world into a global system designed to serve human needs. Animals are constructed as providing goods to humans, and the ecosystems they live within are described as providing waste disposal services ("ecosystems process waste, render it harmless to humans" 75). However, in return for their goods and services, animals receive only toxins, confinement, or death, which is where the economic model breaks down. There seems to be very little consideration of the services humans must necessarily *provide* to others (including other animals) within the ecosystem in order for the ecosystem as a whole to survive.

It is informative to ask "where are the animals?" in Daly and Farley's (2004) discourse. Two quotations that are particularly revealing, are as follows:

- Waste has a direct impact on human well-being and further diminishes ecosystem function. (109)
- First, accumulating toxins have direct negative effects on humans. Second, the toxins damage ecosystems and degrade the ecosystem services on which we depend. (119)

In both of these quotations, animals are part of "ecosystem function" or "ecosystem services," but the negative effects of waste are considered only in relation to humans. Only occasionally are other species talked about as if they mattered for their own sake, in examples such as "Many fish species have dangerously high levels of mercury and other metals, which cause human birth defects and worse when consumed, not to mention their impacts on other species." (Daly and Farley 2004: 120).

There is no doubt that the discipline of ecological economics provides an important new direction for economists, encouraging them to include in their considerations the effects of economic activity on ecosystems, with great potential to oppose ecologically destructive discourses. However, in terms of reconstructing the relationship between humans and other animals, discourse along the lines of Daly and Farley (2004) fails to transcend the anthropocentric assumptions of oppressive discourses, which consider animals only in terms of their use to humans. It is hard to imagine empathy with a "biotic component," a "biotic resource," a "raw material," or a unit of "natural capital."

THE DISCOURSE OF CONSERVATION

Conservation discourse shares some aspects of scientific ecology but plays a particularly prominent role in influencing relationships between humans and animals because of the intense publicity it gains through organizations such as

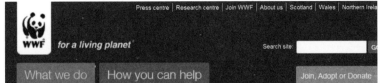

WWF
for a living planet

Search site: [   ] G

What we do | How you can help | Join, Adopt or Donate

Safeguarding the natural world

Wildlife

Illegal wildlife trade
African elephants
African rhinos
- Amur leopard
Asian elephants
Asian rhinos
Dolphins
Giant panda
Iberian lynx
Marine turtles
Mountain gorilla
Orang-utan
Polar bear
Snow leopard
Tigers
Whales
Namibia

Forests

Rivers and lakes

Oceans

+ Tackling climate change

Amur leopard

About the species

The population and distribution of the Amur leopard has been reduced to a fraction of its former size. It is estimated that 80% of its range was lost between 1970 and 1983. Today, the majority of Amur leopards live in the temperate forests of the Primorskii region of Russia – a 5,000 sq km area between Vladivostok and the Chinese border – with a few individuals living in the Jilin and Heiongjiang provinces of NE China, and possibly a few in North Korea.

The Amur leopard, also known as the Far East Leopard or Manchurian Leopard, is listed as Critically Endangered in the International Union for Conservation of Nature's Red List of Threatened Species. With only around 35 left in the wild, it is considered the world's most endangered cat.

The Amur leopard can be distinguished from other leopard subspecies by the widely spaced rosettes with thick borders on its coat.

Challenges and threats

One of the most significant threats facing the Amur leopard is loss of its forest habitat due to logging, forest fires and the conversion of forest for agriculture. In addition, the WWF. There is an interesting tension between the goals of conservationists (often referred to as "broad" or "deep") and the discourse used in communicating with the public. Hails (2007) describes how the WWF was launched:

> The British appeal of WWF was launched with pictures of black rhinos in Africa under the headline "doomed," and Peter Scott had taken George Waterson's sketches of the giant panda Chi-Chi, then residing in London Zoo, and turned it into the logo of the organisation. Chi-chi was the only giant panda residing in the West, had arrived from the mysteries of communist China, and was an evocative species symbol for the challenges facing those concerned with the preservation of wild nature. So despite some deeper thinking which underpinned it, the early days of WWF were ones which were dominated by a preservationist agenda for species and habitats, based on popular appeal. (367)

As discussed in chapter 6, the danger with a focus on preserving a few appealing species is that if taken to the extreme it could result in the protection of small enclaves where rare species live while the rest of the planet is cut, concreted over, or burned. This is clearly self-defeating, both because enclaves are not capable of supporting the genetic diversity necessary for the long-term survival of species and also because large numbers of other species would become rare in the meantime.

For the sake of rare species, currently common species, and humans, it is the broader natural systems that need to be the focus rather than individual species. This was acknowledged in a significant discursive shift occurring in the WWF in 1985 when "WWF formally re-registered its name as World Wide Fund for Nature, to try and escape the preservation of animal species image and reflect a broader view of the situation" (Hails 2007: 367). Now the WWF undertakes a wide range of activities from species protection and protection of forests, rivers, and oceans to tackling climate change and helping people change their lifestyles to reduce consumption. The global website sums up the goal of the organization succinctly:

WWFs ultimate goal is to build a future where people live in harmony
with nature (WWF-Global 2010).

and the UK website offers the following perspective on the educational aims of
the organisation:

We would like education to be based on our interdependent relationship
with nature and the health of our planet, and the life-enhancement and
joy that can be had from appreciating this relationship. (WWF-UK 2010
education section)

The WWF-UK website itself provides a form of informal education for all
those who view it, so it is informative to examine the discourse of the website to
see what kind of relationships it establishes between humans and other animals.
The focus here is on WWF-UK, but it is important to point out that there are
individual websites for WWF in other countries, each using a different mix of
discourse. The main discourses used in the UK site, however, do appear in modified forms across many of the other websites, and, indeed, across the websites of
other, similar organizations.

The information structure of the WWF-UK website gives important clues
as to how issues have been prioritized. Normal reading order (in English) is
left to right, top to bottom, meaning that items placed in the top left are given
highest priority, and there can be a sense of narrative continuity from left to
right. In the WWF-UK website the panda logo is in the extreme top left, with
the strap-line "for a living planet." Below it are three large tabs running from
left to right "What we do," "How you can help" and "Donate" with an arrow
after it, suggesting a narrative and guiding the reader from finding out what
the organization does toward donating. This is important, since it shows that
encouraging people to donate money is a primary goal of the website, and possibly a goal that leads to simplification of educational messages embedded in
discourse of the website.

The top item on the left under the "What we do" tab is "Safeguarding the
natural world," and the top item within this option is "Wildlife." The Wildlife
section in turn consists of a list of species that can be individually clicked on:

> African elephants, African rhinos, Amur leopard, Asian elephants, Asian
> rhinos, Dolphins, Giant panda, Iberian lynx, Marine turtles, Mountain
> gorilla, Orang-utan, Polar bear, Snow leopard, Tigers, Whales (WWF-UK
> 2010)

This information structure shows that the original focus of the WWF on preserving appealing species has been retained in top priority position, with other
aspects such as forests, rivers, and oceans coming after wildlife in the "Safeguarding the natural world" section, and the broader concerns of "Tackling
Climate Change," and "Changing the Way We Live" coming only after "Safeguarding the natural world."

It is clear that the species highlighted in the prime "wildlife" section on the
website are selected on a nonscientific basis of cultural appeal: "As charismatic
icons, species also provide unique opportunities for promoting and communicating critically important conservation and environmental issues" (WWF-UK
2010). The U.S. website is more explicit in linking what it calls "flagship species" with fund raising:

> Our conservation efforts are directed towards *flagship species*, iconic ani-
> mals that provide a focus for raising awareness and stimulating action
> and funding for broader conservation efforts in our priority places; and
> *footprint-impacted species* whose populations are primarily threatened be-
> cause of unsustainable hunting, logging or fishing. (WWF-USA 2010)

Despite the clear selection of "flagship" species on affective criteria, however,
the discourse used in describing the species in the WWF-UK site is very objective sounding, that is, scientific-based discourse scrubbed clean of sentimental-
ity or evaluative statements. The following is prototypical of the discourse used
to describe species across the wildlife section (see figure on page 69):

> The population and distribution of the Amur leopard has been reduced
> to a fraction of its former size. It is estimated that 80% of its range was
> lost between 1970 and 1983. Today, the majority of Amur leopards live
> in the temperate forests of the Primorskii region of Russia—a 5,000 sq

km area between Vladivostok and the Chinese border. . . . The Amur
leopard can be distinguished from other leopard subspecies by the
widely spaced rosettes with thick borders on its coat. (WWF-UK 2010:
wildlife section)

The modality is extremely high, with facts presented baldly as entirely certain,
with the occasional uncertainty expressed using the passive voice of science "it
is estimated that." The selection of information given consists of the kind of scientific facts useful to conservationists: population, distribution, and the physical characteristics necessary to distinguish a subspecies from other subspecies.

The collective nouns *species, subspecies, population,* and *subpopulation* are used
frequently throughout the descriptions of the endangered animals, and animals
are referred to using mass nouns (e.g., *the Amur leopard*) rather than count nouns
(*Amur leopards*). Discourse conducted at the level of mass and collective nouns
has the potential side effect of distracting attention away from direct relationships with individual animals: an individual can be seen, heard, and empathized
with, but a "species" cannot. The scientific abstractions of the discourse of conservation can, of course, play an important role in saving members of endangered species from extinction, but by definition, these animals are few and far
between. If only "species" are to be saved, then the discourse of conservation
has nothing to say about confining, hurting, or killing animals in ways that do
not threaten the species as a whole. There is a degree of separation, therefore,
between species conservation and developing relationships of respect with animals in general.

In some of the species descriptions there is extra information given in a
"natural history" informative style that provides facts that are not strictly necessary in terms of identification and categorization of subspecies, for example:

Dolphins' echolocate by producing clicking sounds and then receiving
and interpreting the returning echoes. From this they can tell the size,
shape, distance, speed and direction of the objects—especially their
favoured food of fish and squid. (WWF-UK 2010: wildlife section)

This extra information does give the reader a wider picture of the animals as a whole, although terms such as "echolocate" indicate that the register is still a disinterested scientific one. This register is used throughout the wildlife section, with terminology such as *range* (as noun and verb), *distribution, fragmentation, habitat,* and *functionally extinct.* In contrast to the "doomed" headlines that accompanied the launch of the wwf, the discourse of the wildlife section puts the endangered status of animals in highly objective-sounding terms, at a remove from the writer:

> The Amur leopard, also known as the Far East Leopard or Manchurian Leopard, is listed as Critically Endangered in the International Union for Conservation of Nature's Red List of Threatened Species. (wwf-uk 2010: wildlife section)

Overall, this discourse enacts a relationship between humans and animals where the human is a disinterested, expert, scientific observer concerned with the facts and statistics necessary to protect a particular selection of species, as well as informing the reader of some of the characteristics of the species being preserved. The animals themselves are primarily members of categories divided up according to physical features rather than being individuals caught up in a life and death battle against the encroachment of humans, with stories of individual suffering or temporary reprieve. The function of this discourse may be to represent the wwf as a science-based organization that can be entrusted to direct funding accurately. However, the distance between humans and animals that disinterested scientific discourse creates may not deliver the educational objective of understanding "our interdependent relationship with nature and the health of our planet, and the life-enhancement and joy that can be had from appreciating this relationship" (wwf-uk: education section).

It is certainly not a joyful discourse, although interestingly, the visual images that accompany the objective-sounding, rational text give out a quite different message. The kinds of images normally associated with analytical texts are charts, diagrams, or bird's-eye views that give disinterested information about populations of animals. Instead, however, the pictures that accompany the descriptions of the species in the wildlife section are very much photographs of individual animals. For the leopard, panda, lynx, gorilla, orangutan, and tiger, the shot is a close-up at "intimate" distance of an individual animal, "demanding" a relationship with the viewer by gazing out of the photo (the "eye-line vectors" meeting the viewer's eyes). For African elephants, dolphins, polar bears and African Rhinos, the pictures "offer" images of individual families, with the vectors showing interaction among family members. Only the turtle is represented in a high-angle, full shot reminiscent more of observation than engagement or empathy.

The visual discourse of the wildlife section is very similar to that of another section of the website, the "adopt-an-animal" section. In the case of the "adopt-an-animal" section, however, the discourse of the linguistic text matches the visual images more closely. The entry on orangutans in this section illustrates this:

> Within the last decade alone, orang-utan numbers have fallen by between 30 and 50%. Help us protect these gentle giants and their forest habitat. (WWF-UK adopt section)

Like the wildlife section of the website this contains some (simplified) statistics and scientific terminology, but unlike the wildlife section it also contains the evaluative "gentle giants" to encourage a more personal relationship between the reader and the animals. Likewise, dolphins are represented as "intelligent, inquisitive creatures," tigers are "the world's largest big cat," elephants are "magnificent," Rhino's are "incredible," and the Amur leopard is "the world's most endangered big cat." While this form of evaluative language may work toward creating affective relationships between people and animals, the question is whether it inspires people to care about species that are not magnificent, incredible, large, or exceedingly rare.

By definition, the animals described in the conservation discourse are rare and so are not ones that readers are likely to come across in their everyday life, except through the "cuddly toy Rhino" that comes with the adoption pack. The scientific based "flagship animal" discourse of the wildlife section and the more sentimental "adopt-an-animal" discourse are clearly effective in fund-raising and raising awareness of a range of issues. However, on their own these discourses seem insufficient to promote a deeper shift, where readers are encouraged to bond with the great variety of species that they interact with both directly in daily life and indirectly through their consumption habits, or to gain a deep understanding of the dependence of their lives on other species.

THE DISCOURSE OF ANIMAL LIBERATION

The animal liberation movement, in contrast to wildlife conservation, focuses specifically on those animals who suffer most at the hands of humans — the ones whose relationships with humans consist of little more than exploitation and abuse. Animal liberation, at first, seems an ideal discourse to promote a radical change in human/animal relationships, yet this discourse too has its limitations. Tester (1991: 196) sums up one limitation by claiming that within the animal liberation movement "The animals are nothing more than objects to which something is done." If this is so, then the discourse of animal liberation is representing only the second of two important aspects. The first is that animals, in their natural state, are conscious beings who can be considered active agents of their own lives, acting according to their nature. The second is that practices such as farming and experimentation remove this ability from them. In other words, a discourse where animals are represented only as passive recipients of cruelty does not challenge destructive discourses that objectify animals and deny their agency.

Animal agency itself is a contentious philosophical issue, discussed in depth in relation to literary studies in Armstrong (2008) and in relation to animal geographies in Philo and Wilbert (2000). There are some theorists who are reluctant to attribute agency to animals at all, ranging from those who view animals as automatons acting only on instinct and incapable of active control over their lives, to those who fear attributing agency is anthropomorphic and therefore does not respect the very different nature of animals. Philo and Wilbert (2000: 18) go some way to attributing agency to animals, advocating a "measured, hesitant and reflected-upon form of anthropomorphism . . . treating *some* animals in *some* situations *as if* they could perceive, feel, emote, make decisions and perhaps even 'reason' something like a human being." They therefore feel licensed to talk about animals

> seeking to stay wild in their wild places, getting on with their own lives and worlds without anything to do with us humans, performing their specific forms of agency to one another, creating their own worlds, their own beastly places, without reference to us. (Philo and Wilbert 2000: 19)

There is nothing anthropomorphic, however, about animals "getting on with their own lives," acting according to their own volition and doing the things they want to do. Undoubtedly this includes perception, emotion, and decision making to different degrees and in different ways for different animals. If agency is considered purely in these terms, then it is possible to analyze the discourse of the animal liberation movement linguistically to reveal who is given agency by the sentence structures involved, and test Tester's claim that animals are treated only as objects.

While there are, of course, many different kinds of texts related to animal liberation, Peter Singer (1985, 1990, 2003) has been extremely influential, and his work provides a prototypical example of at least one major thread in the broader discourse of animal liberation. It is useful to analyze one particular text — *Ethics and the New Animal Liberation Movement* (Singer 1985) — in some detail, because it consists of an overview of the philosophy of animal liberation using a form of discourse that is widespread within the movement. The text contains statements such as:

> Why do we lock up chimpanzees in appalling primate research centres . . . yet would never think of doing the same to a retarded human being at a much *lower* mental level? The only possible answer is that the chimpanzee, no matter how bright, is not human, while the retarded human, no matter how dull, is. This is speciesism. (Singer 1985: 6)

This extract presupposes a form of interaction in which people use a moral calculus to decide how to treat animals by thinking about how they would treat humans in comparable conditions. In terms of relationships, this implies conceptualizing animals in human terms rather than treating animals with respect for who they are. Singer makes an important moral point, but the discourse it is made in seems to be more about humans than about animals. Within Singer's text there are, in fact, 246 references to humans compared to only 96 references to animals. And when animals are mentioned, they are usually (89 percent of the time) referred to in the abstract (e.g., "animals," "those not of our species" or "other creatures").

Tester's claim that animals are represented in animal liberation discourse as nothing more than objects to which something is done is partially borne out by the grammatical constructions used in Singer's text. There are twenty cases in the text where animals appear as grammatical objects, mostly as the affected participants of material processes (actions, deeds) carried out by human agents (see Halliday 2004, Goatly 2000). And as expected, these material processes frequently involve abuse: the human agent "treats animals cruelly," "deprives pigs of room," "poisons rats," "locks up chimpanzees," "confines cows," "uses nonhuman animals," "experiments on monkeys," "captures wild animals," "takes the life of a fish," "kills a fish," and so on.

Equally often, however, animals appear as grammatical subjects (in twenty cases), for example: "animals have rights," "animals were property," "other creatures have interests," "the chimpanzee is not human," "cows like lush pastures," "nonhuman animals suffer," "fish do not have a clear conception of themselves." The pattern is clear, though: none of the processes that animals are the subject of are material processes—they are not portrayed as actually doing things. Instead, these processes are relational, existential, and mental, with the mental processes of animals being illuminated only in so far as they "suffer," or denied, in terms of fish represented as not possessing a "clear conception."

Where are the animals in the discourse of animal liberation? Buried in generic terms, grammatically realized as objects, or the subjects of nonmaterial processes, and often embedded in noun phrases (e.g., "the interests of nonhuman animals," "animal liberationists"). This represents the grim reality of intensive farming, where animals are in fact denied agency and are pushed out of mind as far as possible. The animal liberation movement strongly resists this treatment of animals, but does not necessarily provide a vision of more harmonious relationships or a discourse that could help create these relationships.

THE DISCOURSE OF ANIMAL RIGHTS

The discourse of animal rights has much in common with that of animal liberation but explicitly calls for legal rights to be established for certain species of animals. An important role of animal rights discourse is in countering one of the main assumptions of oppressive discourses: that humans are superior to all other species because of the uniqueness of their intellect, language ability, self-conception, or other arbitrary characteristics. To counteract belief in the uniqueness of humans, statements such as the following frequently appear in the discourse of animal rights:

> They [animals] practice agriculture. . . . Ants construct special chambers containing fungus and bring leaves to nourish it. . . . Animals can make tools: chimpanzees shape sticks . . . bees convey information about the . . . quality of nectar. . . . Animals possess . . . the power to deceive others! Plovers will feign a broken wing to lead predators away . . . chimps can negotiate mazes . . . great apes possess the ability to learn and to express thought in human forms of discourse. (Gold 1995: 29–30)

Unlike the discourse of animal liberation, animals are represented here as active participants — as agents of material processes. The material processes in which the animals are engaged, however, are the kinds of activities that humans carry out on a scale or to a degree much larger than other animals.

Discourse such as this is based on an assumption that is the same as that of the oppressive discourses it is countering: that superiority lies in the ability to perform arbitrary tasks such as speaking, solving intellectual puzzles, or making tools. While the attempt is clearly to show that humans are not unique, this form of discourse perpetuates the biased criteria that oppressive discourse gives for judging superiority, while still rendering animals inferior because of their lesser ability to perform these tasks. Chimpanzees may be able to make tools, but if this is the criteria for judging superiority, then humans will still be superior since their tools (e.g., fighter planes) are more sophisticated.

If the assumption that animals should be judged in terms of their (minimal) ability to mimic humans in some area is rejected, then people may learn to listen to other animals, and appreciate them for the way they perform the tasks at which they are far more adept than humans. Some animals are expert at searching for warm air currents on which to soar effortlessly in the sky; others create a social map through surrounding smells; still others have an amazing sense of direction; most are, quite unlike humans, masters of living sustainably in the local environment.

The essence of animal rights discourse is that it is illogical to cause suffering to animals because there are no relevant differences between humans and (at least some) other animals that could justify the difference in treatment. However, the emphasis on logic has been criticized for being excessively rationalist (Donovan 1993: 168). Indeed, Regan's (1985) *The Case for Animal Rights* attempts to create distance from emotion and sentiment, despite the fact that these (rather than logic alone) form the basic building blocks of good relationships. Regan writes:

> Since . . . we must recognise our equal inherent value as individuals, reason—not sentiment, not emotion—reason compels us to recognise the equal inherent value of these animals and, with this, their equal right to be treated with respect (Regan 1985: 24)

This exhibits what Donovan (1993: 168) calls an "inherent bias in contemporary animal rights theory towards rationalism, which, paradoxically, in the form of Cartesian objectivism, established a major theoretical justification for animal abuse." In this way, animal rights discourse uses some of the same tools as oppressive discourses, but for diametrically opposite ends. By focusing attention away from "emotion," the discourse of animal rights has the potential to discourage sensitivity toward, compassion for, and emotional connection with the plight of animals.

The rationalist approach also makes animal rights discourse susceptible to counterattacks that attempt to dismiss the whole foundation of the movement by mimicking and disrupting its basic logic. For example, Lomborg (2001), who sets out to show that the state of the world is improving, has a vested interest in ignoring the ever-increasing suffering of animals. He uses the same kind of logical discourse as animal rights, but with the opposite goal of excusing his exclusion of animals in his assessment of the state of the world:

> While some . . . people will definitely choose to value animals and plants very highly, these plants and animals cannot to any great extent be given particular rights. . . . Should penguins have the right to vote? . . . If we use the inalienable rights argument we could not explain why we choose to save some animals at the bottom of the sea while at the same time we slaughter cattle for beef. (Lomborg 2001: 12)

This treats animals as tokens or categories to be manipulated for the sake of making a logical point, rather than as sentient beings. The discourse of animal rights is very susceptible to attacks of this type because if how we should treat animals is just a matter of logic, then it is easy to come up with a logical sounding justification for treating them badly.

———————————

Looking at the extensive research available on other oppressive discourses, such as those of sexism, racism, and ableism, there is a clear pattern to the way exploitative discourses are resisted. When enough attention is focused on the oppressive nature of a particular discourse, a counter-discourse arises and is adopted with enthusiasm by activists. At first, the counter-discourse appears to offer the path to liberation, but gradually it becomes clear that it does not completely break away from the assumptions of the oppressive discourse or provide a complete solution. An example is the highly oppressive medical model of disability, which was vigorously resisted with a new discourse (the "social model") in ways that had huge benefits for the disabled population. The social model was the main focus of disability activists for a long time before its limitations were exposed and researchers started looking in new directions, but never backward to the oppressive medical model (Crow 1996).

Discourses of oppression have a built-in resilience through their employment of categorical phraseology that gives the sub-message that "This is the one-and-only possible Truth." To oppose such discourses, counter-discourses often make use the same kind of authoritarian presentation, since this style is more likely to be published and prove influential. The problem is that if and when counter-discourses succeed, they too become resilient, and it becomes difficult to transcend them with new discourses that address their shortcomings. Singer's discourse, for example, has changed little in thirty years (see Singer 2003), and still has a central place in the animal liberation movement. In fact, all the counter-discourses described above follow resilient ways of writing to greater or lesser extents. For instance:

> What's wrong—fundamentally wrong—isn't the details that vary from case to case. . . . What's wrong isn't the pain, the suffering. . . . These compound what's wrong. . . . But they are not the fundamental wrong. The fundamental wrong is the system that allows us to view animals as *our resources*. (Regan 1985: 3)

This extract uses categorical assertions of fact, with no hedging of the kind "one way to think about this," or "potentially," or "from one perspective" (see Fairclough 2003a: 41). This way of writing poses a strong challenge to the oppressive discourse, but it closes down the space for alternative discourses to challenge the assumptions of the writer. For example, the use of the expression "the fundamental wrong" rather than "a fundamental wrong" is not open to the possibility that other discourses in the future may describe other fundamental wrongs.

New discourses will arise, but the categorical style of writing means that they will have to challenge and compete, rather than coexist and complement. As Tester (1991: 13) points out, different factions of the animal rights movement have been "refighting the quarrel between Tweedledee and Tweedledum" for a long time. There is a danger, then, that counter-discourses simply provide new orthodoxies that are not responsive to the changing conditions of the world.

The main similarity between oppressive discourses and the counter-discourses that oppose them, is the tendency to treat both human and other species of animals within socially constructed realities, rather than engaging with the lived reality of the animals themselves. Animals are considered to be resources, species, subspecies, varieties, subpopulations, objects of abuse, moral categories, possessors of rights, or entities whose value lies either in rarity, size, or in their ability to mimic human behavior. But despite providing important opposition to oppressive discourses, these counter-discourses do not necessarily encourage an attitude of approaching other animals with respect and with a willingness to see the world from their perspective. While this chapter provided an overview of a range of counter-discourses, the next two chapters provide more detailed analysis of the important counter-discourse of ecology consider alternative discourses that represent animals in very different ways.

5

THE CURTAILED JOURNEY
OF THE ATLANTIC SALMON

This is a chapter about fish, their representation in discourse, and how this could potentially influence how they are treated. It is about the journey of Atlantic salmon, which in the wild would involve swimming far out into the Atlantic, but is increasingly being curtailed by the net walls of aquaculture cages in fish farms. And it is about the relationship between humans and other animals in general, and how we value that relationship. The first section starts by describing some of the consequences that aquaculture has had on salmon and the ecosystems they are part of, and describes how discourse may play a role in how people treat salmon. Of particular importance is the degree to which discourses represent fish as intrinsically valuable, or as valuable only in terms of their utility to humans. The second section analyzes the representation of fish in the Millennium Ecosystem Assessment report, focusing on the extent to which the linguistic structuring of the report represents fish in ways that recognize their value. The third section discusses what a discourse that treats fish as inherently valuable, as animals leading their own lives for their own purposes, might look like, using the discourse of marine biologist and popular science writer Rachel Carson as an illustration.

FISH, ECOLOGY, AND INTRINSIC WORTH

"Salmon farming is a relatively new occupation," says Scottish Quality Salmon (2005), "and of course we have learned to do things better during a steep learning curve." The "learning curve" for salmon aquaculture around the world has indeed been steep, involving lessons about how diseases quickly spread through populations of confined salmon, and beyond, to infect wild salmon: "The salmon parasite, Gyrodactylus salaris, has destroyed wild salmon populations in 44 Norwegian rivers" (Peeler and Murray 2004: 322). Other diseases the aqua-culture industry has learned about the hard way are *infectious salmon anemia virus* (Kibenge et al. 2004), and *infectious hematopoietic necrosis virus* (Miller et al. 2004). To prevent disease, chemotherapeutics such as oxytetracycline are added to feed (Capone et al. 1996), a chemical that has been found to cause spinal deformities (Toften and Jobling 1996).

The learning curve included discovery of how salmon escaping from farms disrupt the genetic makeup of wild populations (Stephens and Cooper 2004) and of how fish waste leads to "toxic and harmful" algal blooms (MacGarvin 2000: 1, Berry and Davidson 2001). The steepest part of the curve was the discovery of how sea lice multiply among the farmed salmon and spread out to wild populations (Butler 2002). The lesions caused by these lice "cause stress and increase the susceptibility of the fish to secondary infections. In extreme infestations, fish can suffer from osmoregulatory failure and death" (Davies and Rodger 2000: 869).

The problems resulting from the confinement of salmon in sea cages (de-tailed in Staniford 2002 and Berry and Davidson 2001) are numerous but do not come as a surprise. There have been many "learning curves" already on land in other intensive animal industries. And the lesson is simple: when we confine thousands, or, on a global scale, billions, of animals in ways that go against their nature, there are serious ecological, welfare, and health repercussions (Turner 1999).

The nature of Atlantic salmon is to hatch in a streambed, grow in the stream, and transform into a saltwater fish, before starting out on a journey. This journey takes the salmon down the river, into the Atlantic, where they can swim as far as Greenland, before returning to the stream they were born in, undergoing yet another transformation of their bodies before they lay eggs again in the streambed and die. Instead of this, farmed salmon hatch indoors, and are then helicoptered in steel buckets to sea-cages where they will spend the rest of their lives confined with thousands of other fish. This is an environment very different from the one they are adapted to thrive in.

The specific problems that occur over time when large numbers of salmon are confined in sea-cages are impossible to predict in advance. Rather than waiting to find out, a precautionary principle of understanding the nature of salmon and violating this nature as little as possible seems to be the most practical way of realizing ecologically sustainable relationships between humans and fish. As Capra (2002: 188) explains, "A sustainable human community interacts with other living systems — human and nonhuman — in ways that enable those systems to live and develop according to their nature."

This is compatible with an age old cultural apparatus that has assuaged ecological destruction before in indigenous cultures around the world: empathy, respect, and compassion for other animals. As McIntosh (2001: 39) points out, "The harmony with nature we have come to associate with settled indigenous peoples has been in part a *learned* harmony. It has been kept in place by technological limitations and totemistic respect for other life and by taboos against disrespect." Without the same technological limitations, respect becomes even more necessary as a way of ensuring that technology is applied appropriately.

The "deep ecology" framework (Naess 1990, 1973), encourages the recognition of the "intrinsic value" of the nonhuman world, and recommends allowing animals and plants to follow their nature as far as possible. This recognition has the potential to act as a safeguard to avoid harm to the animals while preventing the ecological damage that inevitably occurs when the nature of animals is violated. The discourse of mainstream ecology, however, frequently denies the intrinsic value of the nonhuman world, not through direct statements, but through the model of the world presupposed by the discourse. The following section analyzes one particular ecological discourse in detail as it is manifested in the key report of the Millennium Ecosystem Assessment (Millennium Ecosystem Assessment 2005).

THE DISCOURSE OF THE MILLENNIUM ECOSYSTEM ASSESSMENT

The Millennium Ecosystems Assessment, conducted at the request of the United Nations, involved the cooperation of more than 2,000 authors and reviewers to produce a detailed statement of the state of the world's ecosystems. The key findings of the assessment were published in the report *Ecosystems and Human Well-Being* (Millennium Ecosystem Assessment 2005), which will be referred to as "the Millennium Ecosystem Assessment Report" or simply "the Report" in this chapter. The assessment was a great achievement and has enormous potential to contribute to the treatment of ecosystems with more care in the future. However, it is important to analyze the report to reveal the extent to which it represents nature, and in this case fish in particular, in ways that assert, or deny, intrinsic worth. The preamble to the Report contains a statement that directly mentions intrinsic value:

> Although the Millennium Ecosystems Assessment emphasizes the linkages between ecosystems and human well-being, it recognizes that the actions people take that influence ecosystems result not just from concern about human wellbeing but also from considerations of the intrinsic value of species and ecosystems. Intrinsic value is the value of something in and for itself, irrespective of its utility for someone else. (Millennium Ecosystem Assessment 2005: v)

This is a deep ecology perspective, but at a distance of three steps: first, there is no direct statement that ecosystems have intrinsic value, only that people are involved in "*considerations* of the intrinsic value." Second, the phrasing "*considerations* of intrinsic value" rather than "*recognition* of the intrinsic value" allows the authors to avoid implying that ecosystems actually do have value. Third, it only mentions the value of "species and ecosystems," rather than the individuals who are part of the ecosystems in question.

The statement at least recognizes that notions of intrinsic value can motivate people to protect species and ecosystems. Since the aim of the Report is to encourage this protection of ecosystems, an important question is: to what extent does the Report itself motivate people to value fish as living beings, to treat fish as intrinsically valuable, through its discourse?

One way to get a clue as to who the Report considers intrinsically valuable is to look at the subjects and objects of the verb "harm" in the Report (i.e., the participant structure of the process of "harm"). For instance:

- Algal blooms in coastal waters are increasing in frequency and intensity, *harming* other marine resources such as fisheries as well as human health. (Millennium Ecosystems Assessment 2005: 9, emphasis added)
- The major problems associated with our management of the world's ecosystems are already causing significant *harm* to some people, particularly the poor (1, emphasis added)

In the first example, "human health" is represented as being affected by algal blooms, but harm to the fish (who suffocate because the algae use up oxygen), is represented only as harm to "marine resources such as fisheries." In the second example, the harm to people is directly stated, but no mention is made of the harm to other species that suffer from "our management of the world's ecosystems."

Analysis of the *affected* participant of the process of "harm" in the Report reveals that it is overwhelmingly humans who are presented as affected. The human *affected* participants in the Report are "indigenous communities," "women," "the world's poorest people," "groups of people," "people," "[human] individuals," "[human] populations," "the poor," and, indirectly, "human wellbeing," "livelihoods," "human health," "[human] populations," and "industry." Where the affected participant is not human, it is most often "ecosystem services" and, in one case, "marine resources," both of which express the nonhuman world only in terms of provisions for humans. Of the ninety-one instances of the word "harm," only four directly represent harm to the nonhuman world — to "native species," "biodiversity" (twice), and "ecosystems" (though never to "fish" or animals as individuals). The Report does not explicitly state that harm to fish is of no consequence, but this ideology is encoded in the discourse through the patterning of the word "harm" — the harm to humans is important enough to be considered worthy of mention, but the harm to any other species is not.

It is significant that in the Report the word "fishery" appears more often than "fish" (110 times compared to 61), revealing how fish are thought of primarily in terms of human industry. This is subtly different from how other animals are represented. For example:

> African mammals, birds in agricultural lands, British butterflies, Caribbean corals, and *fishery species* show the majority of species to be declining in range or number. (35, emphasis added)

In this example, the decline of mammals, birds, and butterflies is expressed as if it is something negative in itself, as if these animals have intrinsic worth. Paralleling "mammal" and "bird" we would expect "fish," but instead we find "fishery species." The same pattern can be seen in Beckerman's (2002: 54) statement that "only special regulations and governmental control can prevent the extinction of many endangered species, such as elephants, rhinos, and *fish stocks*." (emphasis added).

Writing of fish collectively in terms of "fishery species" could have the effect of making the fish themselves, as individual animals leading their own lives, invisible. Another linguistic device that can have a similar homogenizing affect is metaphor, for instance:

- Currently, one quarter of marine fish *stocks* are overexploited or significantly *depleted*. (41, emphasis added)
- The fish being *harvested* are increasingly coming from the less valuable lower trophic levels as populations of higher trophic level species are *depleted*. (15, emphasis added)
- Trade in *commodities* such as grain, fish, and timber . . . (59, emphasis added)

In the first and second examples, fish are treated as "stocks" that can be "depleted," representing wild fish in economic terms as human property. In the third example, fish are represented as a commodity, and equated with grain and timber. The parallel between "fish" and "grain" ties in with the metaphor of "harvest" in the second example. This metaphor euphemistically disguises the death of the fish, as do other euphemisms within the Report, such as "removed," "caught," "captured," "landed," or "eliminated," all of which refer to the killing of fish.

The morphology of the word *fish* is such that it is impossible to tell from shape alone whether the word is a count or mass noun. However, in the third example, the parallel with the mass nouns "grain" and "timber" (as opposed to trees) shows clearly that "fish" is being used as a mass noun, representing fish en masse rather than as individuals. Dunayer (2001) suggests that the word *fishes* can restore individuality, but in the Report the word is only used twice, and in ways that refer to different *species* of fish rather than individuals ("the biomass of some targeted species, especially larger fishes," 117).

More detailed consideration of grammatical patterning in the Report further confirms the tendency to avoid acknowledging fish as animals who are living and losing their lives. This grammatical patterning is summarized in table 5.1, which includes all cases of the word *fish* mentioned in the Report.

Table 5.1 reveals how rarely fish, in themselves, are participants in verbal processes — only four times out of sixty instances (as carrier/affected participants toward the end of the table). When they appear in clauses they are usually embedded in noun phrases (e.g., "quantity of fish," "use of fish"), often as the modifier of the noun (e.g., "fish demand"). The underlying verbal process behind "fish demand" is "people demand fish," but the people are removed from consideration through the nominalization of "X demands Y" to become "Y demand." Importantly, there are no verbal processes that represent fish as doing things for themselves; things like swimming, eating, suffering, or dying. When the death of fish is implied, the agent is always missing (fish catch, fish harvest, fish kills, fish landings, overharvest of fish, the catch of fish, capture of fish). What is being described in the Report is the relationship between fish and humans, but through the disguise and deletion of the agent, the relationship is represented in the absence of humans.

With only one exception, all of the grammatical patterns of clauses involving fish in the Report represent fish as economic commodities rather than as animals with intrinsic value. The one exception is the following:

TABLE 5.1 Grammatical Analysis of *Fish* in the Millennium Ecosystems Assessment (2005)

MODIFIER OF NOUN	INSTANCES
fish catch	6
fish stocks	6
fish consumption	4
fish production	4
fish population(s)	3
fish products	3
fish species	2
fish kills	2
fish harvest	2
fish landings	1
fish demand	1
fish supplies	1
fish productivity	1
fish feed	1
fish biomass	1
fish nursery	1

EMBEDDED IN NOUN PHRASE	INSTANCES
demand for fish	3
the overharvest of fish	2
services such as fish	2
quantity of fish	2
capture of fish	2
use of fish	1
the catch of fish	1
reliance on marine fish	1
products such as meat, fish	1
commodities such as fish	1

EMBEDDED IN ADJUNCT	INSTANCES
degraded habitat for fish	1

CARRIER PARTICIPANT OF ATTRIBUTIVE PROCESS	INSTANCES
fish at higher trophic levels are of higher value	1

AFFECTED PARTICIPANT OF MATERIAL PROCESS	INSTANCES
the fish being harvested	2
capturing more fish	1

The potential consequences include eutrophication of coastal and fresh-water ecosystems, which can lead to *degraded habitat for fish* and de-creased quality of water for consumption by humans and livestock. (69, emphasis added)

The expression "for fish" in "degraded habitat for fish" represents degrading as something that directly, and negatively, affects the lives of the fish them-selves, according them a measure of intrinsic value. This stands in contrast to statements that describe pollution only from a human perspective, such as the following:

> Toxic chemicals produced by some blue-green algae during blooms keep people from swimming, boating, and otherwise enjoying the aesthetic value of lakes. (70)

Overall, the discourse of the Millennium Ecosystems Assessment Report does not explicitly devalue the lives of fish, but with very few exceptions fails to ac-cord them intrinsic value, representing them en masse as commodities.

IDEOLOGY, HEGEMONY AND INTRINSIC WORTH

In reaction against the devaluing of nonhuman life inherent in "shallow ecol-ogy," the first platform statement of deep ecology states explicitly:

> The well-being and flourishing of human and nonhuman life on Earth have value in themselves (synonyms: intrinsic value, inherent worth). These values are independent of the usefulness of the nonhuman world for human purposes. (Devall and Sessions 1985: 70)

Luke (2002: 184) criticizes deep ecology, however, for being idealistic:

> Political action is pushed off into the realm of ethical ideals. . . . Without real opportunities to change collective activity — in the economy, ideol-ogy, technology, or polity, this . . . might be, at best, a green quietism.

Whether deep ecology is a form of quietism or not depends partly on whether its ethical ideals find their way, through intertextual transfer, into official documents that have an influence on policy making. In fact, there is evidence that the ideas of deep ecology *are* finding expression in documents that are at least close to being widespread and official. One example is the Earth Charter, which has been adopted by a large number of institutions, though not yet by the United Nations. This charter offers a commitment to "recognize that all beings are interdependent and every form of life has value regardless of its worth to human beings" (Earth Charter 2005: 2). Another example is the UK Sustainable Development Commission, which used to report directly to the United Kingdom government, and stated:

> Even as we learn to manage our use of the natural world more efficiently, so we must affirm those individual beliefs and belief systems which revere Nature for its intrinsic value, regardless of its economic and aesthetic value to humankind. (Sustainable Development Commission 2005)

Even the Millennium Ecosystem Assessment Report states the following:

> Ultimately, the level of biodiversity that survives on Earth will be determined not just by utilitarian considerations but to a significant extent by ethical concerns, including considerations of the intrinsic values of species. (Millennium Ecosystem Assessment 2005: 58)

All of these statements are using the terminology of the deep ecology movement. However, as we have seen, the discourse of the Millennium Ecosystem Assessment Report constructs fish in ways that go against the professed concern with intrinsic worth. And this leads to an important point. In order to encourage recognition of the intrinsic value of fish, it is not enough just to state that "fish have intrinsic value." Such statements lead to a great deal of philosophical discussion of whether fish objectively have that value in themselves, whether it requires a human observer to notice that value, or how it could be rationally proven that fish have intrinsic value (Light and Rolston 2003). This is reminiscent of similar discussions of the intrinsic value of humans during times of slavery before the idea that humans are intrinsically valuable became widespread and commonplace.

In the end, much of ethics comes down to a struggle for ideology to be naturalized (see van Dijk 1993). The idea that all humans have intrinsic value has been naturalized across a wide range of discourses, meaning that it is assumed as a taken-for-granted and obvious fact about the world, rather than something to be discussed or asserted. An example of this would be: "The degradation of ecosystem services is harming many of the world's poorest people" (Millennium Ecosystems Assessment 2005: 27). The Report does not explicitly state that poor people have intrinsic value and that harming them is a bad thing, but takes this as a completely commonsense assumption (see Fairclough 1989: 70). Likewise, ecological discourse could help to instil a sense of the intrinsic worth of the more-than-human world through discourse that treats it as plain commonsense that other species actively lead their own lives and that harm to them is something negative in itself, to be avoided as far as possible. For many, this is indeed common sense and obvious, but the discourse of the Report shows how the world can be represented in ways that deny this.

RECOGNIZING INTRINSIC WORTH: *SILENT SPRING*

An important question is, what would an ecological discourse that did implicitly recognize the intrinsic worth of fish look like? An example can be found in the writings of the marine biologist Rachel Carson, particularly in her seminal work *Silent Spring* (Carson 1962). This book, more than any other, helped to raise consciousness about the ecological crisis and found the environmental movement. There are no explicit statements within the book claiming that fish or other animals have "intrinsic value," or need to be respected or empathized with. Despite this, there is something about her writing that manages to present fish as valuable in themselves, as sentient beings leading their own lives. Analysis of the discourse of *Silent Spring* can help reveal what this "something" is.

In places, Carson (1962) describes the effects of ecological destruction for humans in much the same way as "shallow" ecological discourses such as the Millennium Ecosystem Assessment Report:

- The invasion of streams, ponds, rivers, and bays by pesticides is now a threat to both recreational and commercial fishing (131)
- The fisheries of fresh and salt water are a resource of great importance, involving the interests and the welfare of a very large number of people. (141)

But in the majority of cases, fish are represented in ways that differ markedly from the Report. First, the harm that pesticides and pollution cause is expressed first and foremost in terms of the fish themselves, not "fisheries" or "marine resources." For instance:

- Toxaphene, a chlorinated hydrocarbon, killed all the fish inhabiting the streams. (51)
- Fishes and crabs were killed in enormous numbers. (116)
- In Pennsylvania, fish were killed in large numbers. (131)

In these examples, fish are the *affected* participant in verbal processes. The agent is not made explicit, but the particular verb is "kill," which at least refers directly to the death of the fish (as opposed to "capture," "catch," "harvest," or "eliminate"). Killing is something that is generally viewed negatively, so this phrasing, together with the fact that human interests are not mentioned, suggests that the killing of the fish is a bad thing in itself.

In the second and third examples, it is unambiguously the count-noun version of "fish" that is used ("large numbers" as opposed to "a large quantity of fish"), highlighting that it is individuals who have been killed. Similarly, the frequent use of the pronoun "they" for fish (e.g., "they had few competitors," 126) represents them as individuals.

In a discussion on cooperation between the forest service and the government, Carson's first concern is with the fish: "But can such cooperation actually succeed in saving the fish?" (129), rather than saving the fishing industry or "fisheries." Carson goes as far as describing fish as "the principal victims"

("Again, fishes and crabs were the principal victims," 138). There is no hiding the fact that the fish die, and the following vividly expresses the loss occurring as they die:

> Dead and dying fish, including many young salmon, were found along
> the banks of the stream. . . . All the life of the stream was stilled. (123)

This wording represents the suffering and death of the fish, and the stilling of life in the stream, as something negative in itself— the underlying model is one that assumes intrinsic worth.

The most noticeable difference between Carson's writing and that of the Millennium Ecosystem Assessment Report is the participant roles that the fish fill. The expression "the fish inhabiting the streams" (51) places "fish" in agentive role, actively leading their lives in the stream. The following sentences likewise give fish a participant role in verbal processes:

- The salmon . . . moved in . . . ascended their native river . . . deposited
  their eggs. . . . These young fed voraciously, seeking out the strange
  and varied insect life of the stream. (123)
- For thousands upon thousands of years the salmon have known and
  followed these threads of fresh water that lead them back to the rivers. (122)

In the first example, the salmon are *agents* of the processes of "moving," "ascending," "depositing," "feeding," and "seeking out"— these are material processes, in active sentences, representing the salmon as sentient beings actively engaged in living their lives. Importantly, the second example makes salmon the *senser* of a mental (cognitive) process of "knowing," representing salmon as conscious beings. This discursive way of constructing fish derives from Carson's earlier writing in *The Sea Around Us* (Carson 2003/1951) and *The Edge of the Sea* (Carson 1999/1955), which focuses on lyrically describing natural history and marine ecology rather than confronting environmental problems. Parallel examples of agency in these earlier books are as follows:

- Through the same openings that admit the light, fish come in from the sea, explore the green hall, and depart again into the vaster waters beyond. (Carson 1999/1955: 118)
- For months or years these fish have known only the vast expanses of the ocean (Carson 2003/1955: 42)

Above all, Carson's writing expresses empathy with the fish. A clear example of this is how, in *Silent Spring*, Carson takes what must have been quite dry, objective data from the Fisheries Research Board of Canada, and represents the information from the perspective of the fish themselves, describing what the fish at the time must have "found":

- Even in the second year after DDT enters a stream, a foraging salmon parr would *have trouble finding* anything more than an occasional small stonefly (124 emphasis added)
- The young salmon hatching in the north-west Miramichi in the spring of 1955 *found* circumstances practically ideal for the survival. (126 emphasis added)
- The salmon fry of that year not only *found* abundant food but they had few competitors for it. (126 emphasis added)

It may seem unnecessary to analyze a discourse (that of Carson's *Silent Spring*) and point out explicitly that it represents salmon as conscious beings living their lives for their own purposes, whose suffering and death is something negative in itself. For many readers, Carson's writing just represents things how they obviously are. However, when looked at in contrast with the Millennium Ecosystem Assessment Report's representation of fish, it becomes clear that this is not the only way of representing fish. The other way uses phrasings and grammatical constructions that make fish, as individual beings, invisible and unimportant, and only mattering collectively as a "stock" or "resource."

In the Report there are no explicit statements denying the intrinsic worth of fish, like the infamous statement from the economist Beckerman (1974: 108): "It is much more useful to think of pollution as existing only in so far as harm is done to human beings. . . . As regards water pollution, for example, we are interested only in mankind, not fishkind." However, by recognizing harm to humans caused by damage to the ecosystems that fish are part of, and not recognizing the harm to fish themselves, the Report seems to be based on a similar, though implicit, ideology.

In terms of social justice in the human world, the Report makes a powerful and important statement, because it presents a world where it is not just *some* humans but *all* humans who have intrinsic worth, and emphasizes that ecological destruction will harm the poor first. However, in terms of presenting models of the world that encourage respect beyond the human world, the Report is limited by its representation of animals and nature.

The extensive ethnographic research into the social construction of salmon among biologists carried out by Scarce (2000, 1997) suggests one possible reason why documents such as the Report may be reticent to acknowledge intrinsic worth. Scarce's argument is that until recently, biologists could study the lifecycle of salmon for its own sake, something that is quite compatible with treating fish as animals with intrinsic value. However, public policy and economic pressures have lead to a situation where biologists can only get funding and recognition if their work is directly tied to commercial interests: "Politics and economics impress upon scientists a new sense of urgency, and these pressures lead to a narrowing cognitive construction of salmon. Even to biologists the salmon become embodiments of public policy and tools for economic gain." (Scarce 1997).

The above analysis of the discourse of the Millennium Ecosystems Assessment Report was sent to the authors of the Report themselves for feedback. The following reply from someone who played a senior role in producing the Report is highly instructive of the tensions that authors face in producing a work such as this:

Extremely interesting! I very much appreciate this type of analysis and also think that the conclusions are quite correct. There is no question but that we framed the assessment in extremely anthropocentric terms and did so quite intentionally in order to explore more explicitly the economic, health, and social connections between ecosystems and people. Although this has its benefits in terms of articulating the issues in terms that many who hold real power can understand (e.g., finance ministers, CEOs of companies, planning ministers), it also has costs in devaluing the intrinsic worth of species as you note. For the audience we were aiming at, that cost was worth paying in my view but ideally in the future assessments might be able to provide a better balance here. (Anon.)

The Report is not an isolated example of a text that treats the nonhuman world in ways that deny its intrinsic worth: it is, rather, an instance of a far more widespread discourse in ecological science. Like the destructive discourses of the animal product industries, the discourse employs a variety of linguistic techniques to deny intrinsic worth in order to appeal to economic and political interests.

How can we prevent repeating the "learning curve" of disease, suffering, and ecological problems that resulted from the curtailment of the journey of the Atlantic salmon? If the deep ecology movement is right, then one of the best ways could be through encouraging recognition of the intrinsic worth of fish in people who directly or indirectly influence their life and death.

This chapter argued that explicit statements declaring that fish have intrinsic value may not be enough to influence social constructions. Instead, discourses that treat the intrinsic value of fish as a taken-for-granted assumption about the world are potentially much more powerful. Rachel Carson has shown how this is possible even within a science-based discourse, albeit one transformed for popular consumption without the rigid constraints of peer-review. With the increasing influence of deep ecology, it may be possible that future ecological discourses will encourage respect for the intrinsic value of fish and other animals. If analyses such as the one above can elicit comments such as "ideally in the future assessments might be able to provide a better balance" from senior authors, then they have the potential to contribute to shaping the future of the discourses they analyze, which is the ultimate aim of discourse analysis.

6

BOYD'S FOREST DRAGON,
OR THE SURVIVAL OF HUMANITY

This chapter continues to explore counter-discourses through detailed analysis of how the term *biodiversity* is used across a wide range of discourses. The aim is to show how one particular word can be used with entirely different meanings in different discourses, depending on the goals and ideologies of its users, and to illustrate the impact that semantics can have on relationships between humans and other animals.

The briefest and most casual observation of the life-forms that inhabit Earth reveals how strikingly diverse they, or rather we, all are. No two people, mice, or blades of grass are identical, and there are enormous gulfs between, say, giant squid, field poppies, and giraffes. Basic biology shows that diversity is not just an incidental property of life but fundamental to how life "works" — to its evolution and its continuing ability to survive. As Haila (1999: 170) puts it "Diversity is both an external characteristic and inherent precondition of living nature." Often overlooked is the fact that similarity is also central to how life works: belonging to the same species means that individuals are closely similar, allowing them to come together collectively to fulfil ecological functions, reproduce, and continue the thread of life (Stamos 2003). In physical reality, then, life exhibits a complex pattern of similarity and difference, made even more complex by the ways organisms interact with each other and their physical environments. This complex reality is surveyed by the limited observational powers of humans both casually and through concerted scientific observation, and the results filtered by ideological goals, models, and the limitations of human thought to form the abstract concept *biodiversity*.

The word *biodiversity* is used in many social arenas, by agents with very different ideological positions, and its worth is measured by a great number of contested calculations involving commercial and aesthetic values. The many meanings, definitions, models, and metaphors of biodiversity seem almost as diverse as the biological reality that the term refers to. Some see this as a problem. Takacs (1996: 99) states, "Biodiversity shines with the gloss of scientific respectability while underneath it is kaleidoscopic and all-encompassing." Hawksworth (1995: 5) feels that it is a "pity" that "the word *biodiversity* means quite different things to different people," and Delong (1996: 738) argues that "a widely accepted fundamental definition of biodiversity is imperative."

The multiplicity of meanings is not necessarily negative though—Pickett and Cadenasso (2002: 7) put a significantly positive spin on the similar diversity of meanings encompassed by the term *ecosystem*, stating that "The ecosystem concept has proven to be immensely flexible and productive." The wide variety of meanings can be seen as an inevitable consequence of attempting to describe something complex (the workings of life) using a system (language/human thought) that is far less complex. Nevertheless, different models of biodiversity can be used to serve different ideological goals: Some may relate to saving as many species as possible from extinction, some to saving the kind of charismatic species that stimulate people to support conservation charities, some may be concerned with the continuing ability of vulnerable countries to grow food in a changing climate, and some may aim to divert attention away from preservation of natural systems to serve narrow commercial ends.

This chapter takes the multifaceted nature of the concept of biodiversity as an inevitable consequence of describing life, but tries to unpack some of the ideology and consequences behind various discursive constructions of biodiversity that are used in different spheres. The examples analyzed come from articles about biodiversity written by ecologists, biologists, sociologists, economists, and journalists, ranging from a newspaper article encouraging readers to build a log pile in their back garden to an academic paper calling for the social evolution of a conservation culture that integrates ecological and human needs.

A useful starting point in analyzing the discursive construction of biodiversity is the framework used by Pickett and Cadenasso (2002) in their analysis of the term *ecosystem*. Pickett and Cadenasso's model consists of three levels: *meaning, model,* and *metaphor*. *Meaning* refers to a single encompassing definition that has a level of abstraction so high that it covers most of the meanings that the term is used with in practice. This definition is generally agreed upon by scientists but "covers an almost unimaginably broad array of instances" (2). *Models* are specific simplifications of the concept crafted in response to "the questions guiding the researcher" as well as "features emerging from the nature of the material system under study' (2) where "scale, process, bounds . . . and dynamics" are specified (8). The final level is *metaphor*, which is used in scientific contexts to generate initial ideas and in public discourse to convey ideas clearly and vividly to readers (8).

This is clearly a simplistic framework, and raises questions about which abstract definition should serve as the basic "meaning" of the term; whether a definition can ever capture "meaning," since meaning depends on the context and audience; and what the relationship between metaphors and models is. Keeping these limitations in mind, the following sections put Pickett and Cadenasso's framework into practice for the term *biodiversity*, adapting and further developing it as necessary.

MEANING

Although it is questionable whether there is one definition that is abstract enough to capture the meaning of the term *biodiversity* in all its uses, we can say for certain that when the term is used in practice it is specific along certain dimensions. Some uses, for example, specify that the term applies to a particular area or ecosystem, whereas others specify the relevant area as a large region or even the whole Earth. Area, then, is one of the relevant dimensions in the "meaning" of biodiversity. One way of producing a comprehensive definition would be to gather all the dimensions used in specific meanings while simultaneously leaving the scale of the dimension open. The concatenation of all the dimensions will cover all the different meanings. This seems to be the approach that UNESCO has taken in the definition used in the Convention on Biological Diversity (UNESCO 2005):

> In essence, biodiversity . . . is a multi-dimensional and multifaceted concept that refers to the diversity (in terms of both the variety and the variability) of all organisms and their habitats, as well as the interrelationships between organisms and their habitats. Biodiversity is thus an integrating expression of many different spatial levels or scales of organization, from genes to landscapes, with each level or scale having three different sets of attributes or components, namely: composition, structure and function. . . . "Biological diversity" means the variability among living organisms from all sources including, inter alia, terrestrial, marine and other aquatic ecosystems and the ecological complexes of which they are part; this includes diversity within species, between species and of ecosystems.

This definition uses the conjunctions "and" and "as well as" to concatenate a large range of dimensions, and quantifiers such as "all" and "both" to leave the dimensions open. There may be other aspects that need to be added to this definition, but theoretically they could be added with more "ands," or if they were incompatible in some way they could be included with the conjunction "or." The end result is a definition that can be generally agreed on because it covers all specific uses of the term.

While this may be theoretically sufficient, the more all-embracing the definition becomes, the less operationally sufficient it becomes, making it hard to put into practice. In specific contexts, when researchers are trying to measure biodiversity, or advocates are arguing for or against a particular policy based on its impact on biodiversity, it would be impossible to consider all the factors mentioned in definitions like the one above. Besides this, the definition does not suggest particular weighting or priorities for the different kinds of variability it includes. Any specific uses of the term will therefore necessarily pick up on a subset of features and combine them into particular models.

MODELS

Models of biodiversity lie behind actual, operational uses of the term and are incomplete and simplified subsets of features structured into a particular configuration. This section describes a few of the key components and structures that appear among the great range of models used in practice. One of the procedures for identifying structures of models is presupposition analysis. So, for example, where the term *biodiversity* collocates (i.e., is in proximity) with terms such as *protect, preserve, enhance, conserve, achieve*, and *restore*, as in "X can help *enhance* biodiversity" there is a presupposition that biodiversity is something positively valued, a good.

The first and most obvious feature of all models of biodiversity is the positive orientation of the term itself. Biodiversity is not a value-neutral measurement of an external analogue in the way that temperature is, but is instead a good, a goal to be strived for, like health. Biodiversity therefore appears unmodified in lists of goods (e.g., "flood protection, biodiversity enhancement, and food security"), and appears in lists of bads only in terms of its loss, harm, damage, or destruction (e.g., "pollution, biodiversity loss, and ecosystem degradation"). Biosimilarity, on the other hand, is only occasionally mentioned, usually as a threat to ecosystems, and very rarely as a fundamental property of members of the same species (e.g., Stamos 2003). The reason for the orientation of biodiversity as a good in opposition to biosimilarity may be as a counterbalance to humanity's obsession with simplification, manifest in clear-cutting, intensive monoculture, and concreting over. As Halffter (2002: 1) states,

> If evolution is the essential characteristic of the living world, diversity
> is therefore evolution's main consequence. Differently to the natural
> world, the social world, our world, tends to simplify the systems, look-

ing for efficiency in satisfactory production. The domination of the most efficient leads to homogeneity.

If taken to the extreme, however, the representation of diversity as the ultimate goal may lead to a focus on saving only a minimally viable number of animals in a particular species rather than ensuring that there are enough members of the species to contribute to the functioning of ecosystems across a wide range of areas.

One of the key dimensions along which models of biodiversity vary is the area that the model encompasses. Two of the definitions collected by Baydack and Campa (1999: 5) refer specifically to the Earth as a whole: "[Biodiversity is] all life forms, with their manifold variety, that occur on Earth" and "the total variety of life on Earth." On the other hand, there are definitions that relate biodiversity to a given area, such as "[Biodiversity is] the variety of life and its processes in a given area" (Salwasser, quoted in Baydack and Campa 1999: 5).

There is an important difference between the ethical consequences of whole-Earth definitions of biodiversity and those of given-area definitions. For a hypothetical farmer who is deciding whether to concrete over a marsh on her property, a given-area definition of biodiversity can be scaled to exactly the size of her marsh. Concreting over the marsh would mean a huge reduction in the local biodiversity of that particular area, which, given the ethical orientation of the concept, would make this action seem negative. On the other hand, with the whole-Earth construction, the farmer only has to consider whether there are any identifiable endangered populations, species, or ecosystems in the marsh. If not, she can happily concrete it over knowing that she probably has not reduced the general biodiversity of the Earth in the process.

When put into practice, given-area models of biodiversity can potentially contribute to the agenda of preserving or enhancing local biodiversity through conservation schemes such as ecological and biosphere reserves and the creation of biodiversity spaces in parks, farms, gardens, and agricultural areas. While this may or may not help preserve globally endangered species or ecosystems, it fulfils the deep ecology movement's goal of providing habitats for a great number of individual animals and plants to lead their lives according to their nature. One example of the term used in this way is: "Build a log pile to encourage biodiversity — it's the ideal habitat for small mammals, amphibians and all manner of insects" (Wildlife 2007). This encourages the enhancement of local biodiversity in a very small area (the log pile) on the basis that it provides a home for a great variety of individuals to live, and that is treated as a good in its own right without consideration of globally rare species.

The given-area model, tailored to specific areas that individuals have control over could, therefore, contribute to what Leopold (1966: 262) calls the "social evolution of a land ethic." Halffter (2005: 144) also advocates a land ethic approach, calling for the "promotion of a culture that would gradually take on the mantle of conservation, making it part of the people's mind set." The given-area model can be used to encourage local participation in biodiversity conservation projects in areas where the species and ecosystems involved are not yet endangered, or endangered species have not yet been discovered.

Models of biodiversity diverge from each other not only along the dimension of area but also at the level of the components considered. The UNESCO definition gives a great number of levels, both above and below the level of species, including the variety of niches that organisms occupy in ecosystem processes. However, biodiversity is often considered only at the species level, particularly in the media where scientific models are simplified and reexpressed for a general audience. The typical images used to symbolize the concept of biodiversity in newspapers and magazines are photographs of charismatic, photogenic endangered species (Väliverronen 1998: 30). Grumbine (1992: 26) points out that despite the wealth of definitions and possibilities, "people tend to focus on the species-population level and discount the other levels. . . . There exists an endangered species act but no endangered ecosystem act" (ibid: 26). Odum (1997: 65) makes a similar point "The word *biodiversity* has become almost a 'buzzword' for our concern over the loss of species."

The lack of willingness to include levels below species in biodiversity models has serious consequences given increasingly rapid changes in climate and other environmental conditions. A species that is highly distributed geographically and contains many genetically distinct subpopulations is far more likely to survive in a changing climate. From a human perspective, this is a particularly important consideration for food crops. Given the enormous reliance on a few species of food crop, conservation of genetic variation of these plants and their wild relatives is essential for food security as the climate changes (Hawksworth 1995: 9). Biodiversity of food crop species is also essential given that supplies of oil are peaking and increasing scarcity of fossil fuel–based fertilizer and pesticides will require increased use of locally adapted agricultural species.

Another important factor that only becomes apparent when within-species variation is considered is cultural diversity. Genetic adaptation is not the only way that species that are geographically dispersed adapt to the local environment: in humans adaptation occurs primarily through culture. As Haila (1999) points out, biodiversity bridges the artificial divide between nature and culture. Preserving cultural diversity, particularly of cultures that have developed sustainable ways of living within their local ecosystems, becomes an important part of preserving human biodiversity if within-species variation is considered. For indigenous and peasant movements, such as the Zapatista movements in Mexico and the Ecuadorian National Confederation of Indigenous Peoples, models of biodiversity that include cultural diversity help them challenge cultural imperialism and the seizing of traditional lands by multinational corporations. On the other hand, models of biodiversity that exclude humans or human cultural adaptation potentially promote the clearing of local people from the land in the name of biodiversity. Halffter (2005: 138) writes:

> For local populations with a strongly rooted culture, biodiversity is a basic component of the natural world in which they live and from which they live. The reasons given by some sectors for the conservation of biodiversity often seem incomprehensible. . . . They have lived for centuries using and interacting with the nature that surrounds them, so why should its conservation exclude their activities?

One answer to the question is simply that traditional models of biodiversity often fail to take humans into account at all, since they are based only on a species level, and humans are not an endangered species.

In the media, species extinction is frequently the way that biodiversity is communicated, even when the topic is the contribution of plant and animal populations to local ecosystem services. For instance, a *Telegraph* article reported the following:

> Extinction in the wild "is danger to humans." Scientists have discovered that the high level of extinction among wild species is making human life more precarious than thought. Humans rely on . . . "ecosystem services": fresh water comes from forest-covered mountains. . . . Losing wildlife, or biodiversity, means pushing these [ecosystem services] systems closer to collapse. (Highfield 2007)

Clearly this extract is not actually about endangered species but the ecosystem services supplied by locally biodiverse areas such as forests. These forests supply ecosystem services whether they happen to contain endangered species or not. As Kareiva and Marvier (2003: 347) point out, with an extinction approach "we risk the folly of allowing major ecosystems to degrade beyond repair simply because they do not provide lengthy species lists." In the same way, the following article "Red List of Endangered Species," expresses human survival in terms of endangered species rather than healthy, biodiverse ecosystems across the world:

> Our lives are inextricably linked with biodiversity and ultimately its protection is essential for our very survival. As the world begins to respond to the current crisis of biodiversity loss, the information from the Red List is needed to design and implement effective conservation strategies. (Eccleston 2007)

In addition to models that directly structure the concept of biodiversity it is also important to consider models that indirectly have an impact on how the concept of biodiversity is operationalized. One of these is the economic model that assumes that there is a limited amount of funding to be used to preserve and enhance biodiversity, and that conservation efforts consist of determining priorities for where the money will be spent. The economists Metrick and Weitzman (1988: 22), for instance, write that "the central task is to develop a cost-effectiveness formula . . . that can be used to rank priorities among biodiversity-preserving projects under a limited budget constraint." This may apply to conservation organizations that operate with discrete projects, but if it is to be effective, the concept of biodiversity needs to be taken into consideration in all projects, from concreting over a driveway and agricultural planning to the creation of climate change legislation. Models such as this tend to focus on specific activities for preserving biodiversity, such as the creation of wildlife corridors, rather than working toward political change to include biodiversity considerations in the whole range of other activities that humans undertake.

METAPHOR

Metaphors are similar to models in the sense that they are constructions that select a subset of components from complex reality and organize them into a simplified structure. The difference is that metaphors base the models on a ready-made structure borrowed from a more concretely imaginable source domain (Lakoff and Johnson 1999). So, rather than explaining all the details of the model of a fund manager selecting priorities for limited funding, the same model could be conveyed by using the source domain of "Noah's Ark." This immediately maps the fund manager onto Noah, conservation areas onto the ark, and climate change and other threats to biodiversity as the biblical flood. Metrick and Weitzman (1998: 23), for example, make use of the metaphor as follows:

> Boarding the Ark is a metaphor for investing in a conservation project. . . .
> Noah wants to have a robust rule in the form of a basic ordinal ranking
> system so that he can board first species #1, then species #2 . . . and
> so forth, until he runs out of space on the ark, whereupon he . . . casts
> off. . . . The utility of each species . . . will be measured as a combina-

tion of commercial, recreational and, yes, emotional reactions to a given species.

Because metaphors make use of concretely imaginable structures (like animals boarding an ark) they fix details that might otherwise be left up to the reader to fill in. In this metaphor, for example, Noah will take *species* onto his ark rather than threatened ecosystems or habitats, since habitats cannot climb the ladder into the ark. In this way, the use of the metaphor forces the reader to think about a species-level model, whether that was the intention or not. Metaphors, with their ready-made structures, provide a very efficient yet often simplistic form for thinking about and communicating models. Väliverronen (1998) refers to metaphors as "boundary objects" that mediate between the complexity of scientific models and their communication to the public.

More than one metaphor can be used to convey the same model. For example, rather than Noah's Ark, Kareiva and Marvier (2003) use a medical metaphor to convey a similar economic model:

> The scale of the crisis is so daunting that conservationists widely accept the need for some sort of triage, where limited funds go to the places where the greatest good can be done (Kareiva and Marvier 2003).

Although both metaphors convey basically the same model of limited funds, the source domains are different, and this can result in different reasoning patterns. In the medical case, patients may be rejected by a triage nurse because their injuries are not immediately life threatening, whereas in the Noah's Ark metaphor any species that are rejected will be consumed by the flood. The specificity of the source domain is not always welcome, and Metrick and Weitzman (1998: 23) go to great lengths to explain that the flood is not as bad as the biblical one and some species will survive without help.

Another metaphor that instantiates the limited funding model is the "biological hotspot" metaphor. An example of this from the *Telegraph* is "As well as over 4000 orang-utans, this biodiversity hotspot is home to 30 other mammal species" (Wood 2007). The model behind the hotspot metaphor is that limited conservation funding should be channelled into threatened areas that have the largest number of species in the smallest amount of space. Kareiva and Marvier (2003: 344) criticize the use of the term "hotspot" by using the same metaphor in a way that extends it and draws out its unwanted logical entailment. If attention is placed only on hotspots, they argue, then there are "huge expanses of the planet that it leaves out in the cold—places we might dub biodiversity 'coldspots.'" Kareiva and Marvier illustrate the relationship between choice of metaphor and the goals of the researcher very clearly:

> The hotspot methodology is logical only if the exclusive goal of conservation is to protect the largest possible number of species in the smallest possible areas. Using hotspots to set priorities comes into question as soon as one considers a broader range of objectives such as maintaining functioning ecosystems throughout the world, . . . preserving spectacular wild landscapes that inspire the human spirit or protecting nature in a way that provides for the wellbeing of people living alongside (Kareiva and Marvier 2003: 346).

Väliverronen and Hellsten's (2002) analysis of the *Guardian* and *New York Times* revealed that the most common metaphors for representing biodiversity in the newspapers were as a "library of life," or a "museum." Within library/museum metaphors, the Earth is mapped onto the library/museum and the species mapped onto books/artifacts. There is a worrying metaphorical entailment (Johnson 1983) of these metaphors: in a library, only one or two copies of each book are necessary to provide the required information, and museums, too, need only one or two artifacts of a particular type. The implication for biodiversity is that so long as there are sufficient members of a species in the world to avoid extinction, the information of that species is safe, so there is no need to protect other members of the species from destruction.

The same model is expressed rather differently when the library transforms into a metaphoric database containing cryogenically frozen animals and plants as its entries: "The Frozen Ark project hopes to save a 'back-up' copy of many species before they are lost. Their genetic codes will be stored in a frozen database" (Kettlewell 2004). This sentence uses the term "species" metonymically to refer to a single genetic "code," as if that is all a species consists of. The metaphoric entailment is that if a species goes extinct, then the stored code could restore the species in the same way as a computer can restore data after a crash. The library, museum, and database metaphor are all compatible with the goals of commercial exploitation of genetic material, since only small numbers of specimens are necessary to extract the required material, but they focus attention away from the task of preserving healthy biodiverse ecosystems where life of all kinds (including human life) can thrive.

A metaphor that is quite different from the library or museum metaphor is the metaphor of biodiversity as a collection of works of art, for instance, "To many people, biodiversity . . . must be retained, just like Mozart's concerts, paintings by Van Gogh, or books by Hemingway" (Martens, Rotmans, and de Groot 2003). Like all metaphors, the specificity of the source domain can lead to unintended consequences. In this case there is the obvious point that not all paintings are as spectacular as Van Gogh's and not all books as captivating as Hemmingway's. The question is, where does the metaphor leave species that are not particularly charismatic? Monbiot writes:

> The problem conservationists face is this: that by comparison to almost all other global issues, our concerns about biodiversity seem effete and self-indulgent. If we are presented with a choice between growing food to avert starvation and protecting an obscure forest frog, the frog loses every time. If climate change is going to make life impossible for hundreds of millions of human beings, who cares about what it might do to Boyd's forest dragon? (Monbiot 2004a)

None of the four metaphoric institutions (a museum, library, database, or art gallery) would suffer much if one unexciting item disappeared. And biodiversity is often presented in the press as a question of jobs and human progress versus an obscure species of newt. The problematic entailment of these metaphors is that in the source domain the books, paintings, and art works are not interacting with each other in ways that ensure the continuance of life, as species do in an ecosystem.

Dismissal of biodiversity conservation as an obsession with keeping uncharismatic and irrelevant rare species alive at all costs stands in stark contrast with statements of ecologists, such as Wilson (1992: 35) who writes, "The larger organisms of Earth . . . owe their existence to biological diversity." The model underlying this use of the term biodiversity includes humans as part of ecosystems, dependent on the diversity and interaction of other organisms for our survival. This alternative model can be conveyed using a variety of metaphors, each adding its own specific characteristic to the concept. One common metaphor is that of the Earth as a space-ship and biodiversity as the life support system, for instance: "biodiversity comprises the variety of life and as such is an essential aspect of the basic life support systems for humans and all other living things" (Diesendorf and Hamilton 1997: 72). This certainly raises the stakes in biodiversity conservation—no longer is it about rare species but the future survival of humanity. Like all metaphors, this one has unwanted entailments coming from the source domain: life support systems are mechanical systems involving static functional parts, whereas ecosystems are dynamic, self-adapting, self-organizing systems that actually include the human "passengers."

An alternative metaphor that does not exclude humans from the larger processes of life is the "web of life" metaphor, usually attributed to Chief Seattle: "Man did not weave the web of life, he is merely a strand in it. Whatever he does to the web, he does to himself." In this metaphor, biodiversity actually becomes this web of life:

> Our planet is literally teeming with life. An amazing variety of habitats, people, plants, and animals—everything from penguins to peas and bacteria to buffalo—are all interconnected in a fragile web of life we call "biodiversity." (Field 2008)

Väliverronen and Hellsten (2002) found that the web of life metaphor rarely appears in the media. The reason they suggest for this lack of popularity is that unlike a burning library or museum, an unravelling web does not "evoke powerful images." However, it could be argued that a library or museum, even one on fire, is not particularly scary because within this image humans could just be standing outside watching with regret. With the spaceship and web-of-life metaphors, humans die as biodiversity disappears, making preservation of biodiversity an act of self-defense.

One final metaphor used frequently in both academic sources and the press is *biodiversity as a commodity*, usually money:

> Every country and region has three forms of *wealth*: material, cultural and biological (biodiversity) (Miller 1999: 11)
>
> The global *stocks* of biological diversity generate a flow of services. (Wood, Stedman-Edwards, and Mang 2000: 1)
>
> [Biodiversity is] a depletable *endowment* from the evolutionary process (Wood et al. 2000: 7)
>
> Britain is a biodiversity superpower *squandering* its species faster than almost any country on the planet (Pearce 2007) [emphasis added in each example]

Money is a dangerous source domain to use in structuring biodiversity, however, since money is something that needs to be spent to be useful — there is no use in storing money in perpetuity. On the other hand, biodiversity needs to be preserved or enhanced to provide sustainable yields of natural resources, ecosystem services such as flood defense, genetic products, waste disposal, or more generally the continuation of life.

Interestingly, Hellsten (2002: 109), found that while scientists preferred metaphors such as *ecosystem health* and *collapsing spaceship Earth*, which tie biodiversity to human survival, journalists focus on biodiversity as *repositories*, *stores*, and *treasuries* of products that could be exploited. It is therefore important to question why the media so often use the whole-Earth/species-level model and the resources, museum, library, and artwork metaphors, all of which separate biodiversity from human well-being and survival.

Economic issues may play a role in this, particularly the relationship between the media, the business interests of billionaire media owners, and the corporations that provide the media's advertising revenue. As Monbiot (2004b) points out:

> A journalist who is concerned about the destruction of the environment will by definition find herself at odds with the prevailing media culture. This is because the interests of the men who own the media don't end with the media. Many of them have a direct financial involvement in dozens of different kinds of business.

Countering biodiversity loss often means moving power away from multinational corporations toward local stewardship of the land, reducing consumption and over-industrialization, and protecting areas from unnecessary development, all of which might not suit media owners or advertisers. The conflict between biodiversity and economic growth is something that Stott (2002), writing in the conservative *Telegraph* newspaper, points out, with a clear emphasis on favoring economic growth at all costs:

> Like biodiversity, another key word from Rio, sustainability is thrown into the argument to block development and growth, to conjure up a return to an imagined, usually rural, Utopia. Ultimately, we need strong, flexible and growing economies. (Stott 2002)

This chapter has taken a brief foray into the wide topic of the discursive construction of biodiversity, describing three levels: *meaning, model,* and *metaphor.* At the top level of description, *meaning,* biodiversity was seen to be a complex concept consisting of a wide range of possible levels and dimensions, and necessarily so because the workings of life are not simple or mechanistic. When operationalized, the concept is simplified into a series of models that specify the areas, components, and levels used within a general orientation of more diversity being better. These models can be expressed directly through specifying their structure in full. However, they can be conveyed more efficiently and vividly through the use of the ready-made structures provided by the source domains of metaphors. The extra level of specification of the metaphors arising from the source domain adds entailments that may (or may not) be helpful.

Counter-discourses frequently use the term *biodiversity*, and this chapter has made it clear that the term can be used to serve a wide range of goals, depending on which models and metaphors are employed. The goal could be saving charismatic species from extinction, saving as many species as possible from extinction, allowing further speciation and evolution to continue, contributing to future food security, enhancing ecosystem services such as flood control and carbon sequestration, preserving habitats and diverse biotic communities so that the Earth can support abundant life, providing biodiverse spaces for human mental health, resisting cultural imperialism, or justifying actions that serve short-term economic interests at the expense of animals and nature.

7

FROM COUNTER-DISCOURSES
TO ALTERNATIVE DISCOURSES

ENVIRONMENTAL EDUCATION IN JAPAN

Until this point, the chapters have focused on critical analysis of discourses originating in the UK and the United States, without consideration of the place in which these discourses were produced or consumed. From this point onward, the book is firmly rooted in one particular country, Japan. There are two reasons for this. The first is that the introduction of Western environmental discourses to Japan through the education system illustrates the problematic transnational nature of counter-discourses. The second is that Japan, as a country that has managed to keep some of its traditional culture alive, provides an opportunity to search for alternative discourses that are based on very different assumptions from both the destructive and counter-discourses of the West.

Around 250 years ago, Kagano Chiyo left her house one autumn morning to draw water, but on arriving at her well found a morning-glory wrapped around the well bucket. Showing a deep respect for the flower she refrained from disturbing it, borrowing water from a neighbor's well. Her seventeen syllable poem composed on the occasion became one of the most widely known haiku of all time:

asagao ni / tsurube torarete / moraimizu

morning glory! / the well-bucket entangled / I ask for water

(in Bowers 1996: 44)

The sentiments expressed in this haiku resonate with the *deep ecology* movement in the West, which holds that "all things in the biosphere have an equal right to live and blossom," that all have intrinsic value (Devall and Sessions 1985: 68). This is far removed from destructive discourses in the West, which label unplanned plants "weeds," condemning them to obliteration by weed-killer. It is also far removed from some counter-discourses of environmentalism, which define nature in terms of natural resources to be conserved for ongoing exploitation by humanity. This chapter explores the counter-discourse of Western environmentalism as it appears in English-language classes in the country that the haiku above emanates from, Japan. This will then be contrasted with the deep ecology embedded within traditional Japanese culture.

In present-day Japan, English-language education is part of the curriculum for all students from middle school through university. At university, the majority of textbooks are written by Western authors, and many of the teachers are native English speakers, providing the majority of students with their first substantial experience of intercultural communication. As Dendrinos (1992) points out, however, English-language textbooks are ideologically laden, and the process of intercultural communication involved in English education has been associated with cultural imperialism (see Phillipson 1992). Textbooks covering environmental issues have become extremely popular in English-language teaching, something that initially appears very welcome given that Japan is one of the most environmentally destructive countries in the world. However, it is important to analyze the discourse of the books in the context of the imperialist tendency of Western textbooks in Japan, asking whether the underlying messages are truly aimed at encouraging environmental sensitivity.

Jacobs and Goatly (2000) welcome the incorporation of environmental education into English-language education, but criticize the teaching materials for not explicitly encouraging participation in environmental protection. There is, however, a more profound level on which ecological education in Japan can be criticized, for what many students are learning in their English classes is not the ecological sensitivity of Kagano Chiyo or the deep ecology of the West, but *shallow environmentalism*.

Shallow environmentalism reacts to ecological destruction by addressing immediate physical symptoms (such as acid rain or depletion of the ozone layer) but refuses to address the underlying cultural, political, and psychological causes. The major assumption behind shallow environmentalism is that it is possible to continue "increasing . . . human populations, technologies, and economies" and deal with the resultant environment problems separately, through surface changes such as recycling, more efficient cars, and technology such as carbon capture and storage to mop up the problems (Henning 2002: 78). If the environmental crisis can be dealt with by technical fixes, then fundamental cultural values, such as the American love of the automobile, for instance, do not have to change—"we will not have to question ourselves, our values, or our world views." (Henning 2002: 78). In the intercultural setting of the English-language classroom, shallow environmentalism suggests that there is no problem in the consumerist ideological values being propagated in English education materials, so long as· the ecological destruction· they are associated with is ameliorated.

This chapter begins by exploring the environmental discourse used in a sample of twenty-six English-language textbooks, all of which are specifically marketed to Japanese universities. The textbooks are authored (or coauthored) by native speakers of English, and are referred to in the analysis as textbook A to textbook Z, with reference details appearing in table 7.1 at the end of the chapter.

SHALLOW ENVIRONMENTALISM IN TEXTBOOKS

Although there is considerable variation in layout and approach across the twenty-six textbooks, instances of a particular genre, what could be called *the genre of shallow environmentalism*, can be found across a wide range of the books. The "Acid Rain" section from textbook B provides a prototypical illustration of this genre. Some key sentences extracted from this section are reproduced below, with numbers added in order to facilitate discussion:

1. As early as 1852, in England, rain with abnormally high acidity was recorded.
2. One of the main causes of acid rain is the increase in sulphur dioxide and nitrogen dioxide emissions, the former from coal-fired power plants, the latter from car exhaust.
3. In the world as a whole, it is estimated that 60% of the sulphur dioxide in the air is released naturally; the remaining 40% is added by humans and amounts to perhaps 100,000,000 tons a year.
4. Although many lakes may have alkaline constituents which protect the water from excessive acidity, in those that do not . . . many types of marine life may be killed.
5. While it is clear that we should cut nitrogen oxide emissions from cars and sulphur dioxide emissions from industry, it is also time to carry out more research to understand the complex reactions caused by increased acidity in rain. (Textbook B, 22–24)

The genre consists of four main elements: an unnatural *phenomenon* (in sentence 1), the *cause* (in sentences 2 and 3), the *damage* (in sentence 4) and the *solution* (in sentence 5). However, the logic is, to use Fairclough's terms, a "logic of appearances" rather than "explanatory logic" (Fairclough 2003a: 95). For a start, the causes mentioned consist of only the most immediate physical factors (in this case, sulphur dioxide and nitrogen dioxide), rather than underlying cultural factors such as consumerism. Secondly, the agents responsible for ecological destruction are elided by the use of nominalizations such as "emissions" (sentence 5), or by ascribing the source of pollutants to "car exhaust" and "power plants" (sentence 2), rather than to drivers of cars or users of electricity. When agents are mentioned, they are often identified only in the vaguest and least specific of terms, for example, "humans" in sentence 3.

Since the causes given are physical ones, rather than cultural ones, the responsibility for providing solutions is allocated only to those with direct control of polluting processes. This is reflected in sentence 5, which encourages "us" to "cut nitrogen oxide emissions from cars and sulphur dioxide emissions from industry" rather than reduce the use of cars or reduce consumption of industrial products. This "mystification and obfuscation . . . of agency and responsibility" (Fairclough 2003a: 13) obscures the economic, political and cultural causes of ecological destruction, thus protecting cultural values from challenge.

The "logic of appearances" is manifest in the semantic relations within the genre, which consist mostly of additive and elaborate relations, rather than causal relations, thus providing an abundance of facts, but a dearth of explanation. The grammar also reflects this in its lack of the kind of hypotactic (embedded) clauses that are usually used for explaining causality at a deep level.

The modalization (the degree of certainty with which propositions are expressed) in the chapter consists of a mixture of categorical assertions of fact, and typical patterns of scientific circumspection ("it is estimated that," "perhaps," "may be"). The categorical assertions lend authority, the circumspection adds scientific credibility, and the conclusion (sentence 5) is expressed at the highest level of Potter's (1996: 112) hierarchy of modalization, that is, as an authoritative expression of fact. The authority of the texts is reinforced further by the fact that they are written in English, a language often considered to be the lingua franca of the world and the language of science (Phillipson 1992).

The authoritative nature of the genre, combined with its lack of intertextuality (the weaving of other voices into the text), closes down the space for dialogue between competing representations. This tendency is further reinforced through a series of assumptions (described below) that assume common ground rather than opening up space for difference (Fairclough 2003a: 41). This establishes a one-way channel of communication where environmental science from the West is disseminated outward to the rest of the world in a monologue rather than a dialogue. One of the roles of a critical analyst is to "dialogize" accounts such as this, that is, to point out their contingent nature, de-privilege them, and place them in a dialogue with alternative, competing accounts. A first step toward this is to analyse the assumptions on which the texts are based, and reveal them for what they are, that is, assumptions, rather than inevitable certainties.

Assumptions generally appear in texts in the form of "presuppositions, logical implications or entailments, and implicatures" (Fairclough 2003a: 40). They are particularly important because they can render "contentious, positioned and interested representations a matter of general 'common sense'" (Fairclough

2003a: 82). The environmental education textbooks not only fail to challenge the political and cultural assumptions that lie behind ecological destruction, but also, in many cases, seem to propagate exactly those same assumptions by uncritically incorporating them in their texts. For example, textbook T claims:

> Much of what humans do with their biological resources — including . . . species harvested from natural populations — depends on our having an accurate inventory of life on Earth (T: 13)

This contains the assumption that other species, and even "life on Earth," are "biological resources," and presupposes that these resources belong to humans ("*their* biological resources"). The assumption that all other life-forms are a human possession *metaphorically entails* (Johnson's 1983 terminology) the idea that humans have the right to treat nature in whatever way they please. This is, according to Devall and Sessions (1985), one of the root causes of ecological destruction, yet it finds its way into environmental educational materials in Japan. Textbook T, therefore, seems not only to be ignoring the political and cultural causes of ecological destruction, but also entrenching them. It is possible to identify similar ecologically destructive assumptions across many of the textbooks, four of which are detailed below.

Assumption 1: Excess Consumption of Resources Improves Quality of Life

The idea that "the more we consume, the happier we become" is, perhaps, one of the most deeply entrenched and ecologically destructive "commonsense" assumptions of late modernity (see Monbiot 2000). It is highly persistent because it is, in Fairclough's (1989: 84) terms, a commonsense assumption "in the service of sustaining unequal relations of power," being tied to narrow commercial and political interests. Many of the environmental education textbooks not only fail to challenge this assumption, but also incorporate it within their discourse, thereby perpetuating it. For example, while discussing the problems of pollution that cars cause, Textbook K states that:

> Simply stated, cars offer fun and freedom. When we get behind the wheel and get on the road, we can flee the monotony of daily life . . .

even if we are forced to spend most of our time sitting in traffic jams,
the allure of the automobile is its promise of escape. (K: 11)

This contains the presupposition that "daily life is monotonous" and just sitting
in a car is enough to escape. The implication of positively charged words like
"allure" is that the escape is to a better, rather than worse condition. Textbook
I, while also mentioning the problem of car pollution, gives a similarly positive
view of cars in general:

Cars . . . are expressions of a person's individuality. . . . An office worker
may go to work in sombre clothes, but on weekends he or she drives
a dashing sports car . . . : the car has released that person's inner self,
which is obviously hidden during the week! (I: 7)

This passage presupposes that people have "inner selves," metaphorically hidden by "sombre clothes' at work, but that can somehow be "released" through
motor vehicles. *Release* necessarily implies going from confinement to freedom,
and in this extract the confinement is associated with work and the negative
adjective "sombre," while freedom is associated with weekends and the positive "dashing." This represents overconsumption as the solution to long hours
of monotonous work, *rather than the cause*. Furthermore, in a discussion of the
benefits achieved in the Netherlands through the promotion of cycling, Textbook (I) insinuates that the love of cars is more important, even, than health
or clean air:

The Dutch say that now their air is getting purer and that their health
is better. But motorists could ask the Dutch one simple question: "Can
you put your hand on your heart and honestly say that you love your
bicycle as much as you love your car?" (I: 7)

These examples blatantly promote consumerism, but there are other, more subtle, ways by which consumerism is encouraged. Textbook R states that:

It is true that we'll be able to enjoy more and more benefits of technological achievements in our daily lives, but at the same time the ex-

traordinary advances in technology will create . . . a lot of undesirable problems on a global scale. (R: 49)

The words "enjoy" and "benefits" evaluate "technological achievements" positively, taking it as an unproblematic assumption that our daily lives will be improved by more and more technology. This shuts out the voices of those who question whether, for example, the move toward genetically modified food, labor-saving devices that remove the necessity for bodily movement, and visual devices that confine people behind screens, really do improve the quality of life. The locus of undesirable problems associated with technological improvements is, instead, placed firmly outside of "our daily lives," somewhere in the "globe" ("on a global scale"). Textbook B provides a similar example:

Our problems come from . . . the current consumer lifestyle. This way of life is *enjoyed* by about 1 billion rich people (B: 1, emphasis added)

In this case, the use of the word "enjoyed," rather than a neutral alternative such as "led," treats the assumption that "consumption is enjoyable" as unquestionable common sense. A related assumption is that reducing consumption is a sacrifice, which appears in Textbook X. Rather than describing the benefits of a materially simpler lifestyle, the textbook insists that "We have to learn to tighten our belts, make sacrifices'" (X: 15).

The assumption that excess consumption leads to happiness, whereas frugality leads to hardship, is not, of course, inevitable, and it would have been quite possible for the textbooks to challenge it in the way that Monbiot (2000) does:

According to the Worldwatch Institute, we have used more goods and services since 1950 than in all the rest of human history. But we still don't seem to be happy. Indeed, over the same period, 25-year-olds in Britain have become ten times more likely to be afflicted by depression. . . . The World Health Organisation predicts that . . . depression will become the second commonest disease in the developed world.

Assumption 2: Nonhuman Life Has No Intrinsic Worth

The harmony with nature achieved by many indigenous peoples around the world is, according to McIntosh (2001: 39), based on "respect for other life and by taboos against disrespect." However, a common thread running through the textbooks is the often subtle, but sometimes obvious, devaluing of animals and other living beings.

This devaluation is most clearly seen in the metaphoric treatment of animals and plants as resources (O'Neill 1993: 3). To give some examples: animals and plants are referred to as "food- and fibre-producing organisms" (T: 1), gorillas are "vulnerable assets" (Y: 29), coral reefs are "underwater supermarkets" (X: 80), trees are "timber resources" (A: 45) and fish are "marine resources" (P: 97).

Textbook T employs the metaphor of an "inventory of life on Earth" (T: 13), thereby construing human activity as a business, with all other forms of life relegated to raw materials. To construct the inventory, specimens of species are collected and "deposited in museums" (T: 9). The same textbook mentions only "museums and zoos" as places where nonhuman life can be encountered:

> The concept of ecosystem is a highly instructional tool with which humans may easily learn a great deal about their planet and significantly enrich their trips to museums and zoos. (T: 42)

This is clearly contradictory, as an ecosystem is a living system of interaction, but animals in zoos and museums are either isolated in cages or dead.

Another way that nonhuman life is devalued is by expressing ecological destruction not as a tragic loss of life or the suffering of huge numbers of individuals, but in terms only of human economic loss. For example:

> The oil polluted thousands of kilometres of coast . . . and killed countless sea plants and animals in important fishing areas. Thousands of people whose jobs depended on clean seas and tourism lost money. (C: 69)

If this extract had stopped after "killed countless sea plants and animals" it would give the message that the lives of the plants and animals, in themselves, are valuable. But it continues, delivering the message that the disaster matters only in its effects on human livelihoods. In the following two extracts, the same effect is created by employing the word "valuable":

> [Because of acid rain] in Quebec, 100,000 square kilometres of *valuable* maple forests have been damaged. (Y: 56, emphasis added)
>
> Millions of tons of commercially *valuable* "by-catch" [dolphins, fish, etc.] are thrown overboard each year. (K: 26, emphasis added)

In many of the textbooks, species are recognized only as a whole, rather than by the individual plants or animals of which they consist. By condemning only the destruction of species, the texts tacitly condone any destructive activity targeted at individuals or populations whose demise does not directly impact the survival of the species. The following examples refer only to *species* or *types*, thus overlooking the effects of ecological destruction on individuals who belong to species that are not (yet) endangered:

> As we clear away the natural habitats of animals . . . we may be destroying various *species* forever. (I: 27 emphasis added)
>
> [Because of acid rain] many *types* of marine life may be killed. (B: 23 emphasis added)

Extinction is defined in terms of a *commercial* tragedy in the following examples:

> Every day about fifty species of plants and animals that could be sources of medicine become extinct. (C: 13)
>
> When we lose a species we lose its unique genes as well as its products. (B: 79)

Another way of focusing attention away from protecting animals and plants as individuals is through the use of superordinate mass nouns such as *by-catch*, *fauna*, *wildlife*, and *marine life*. Textbook C measures the "amount" of *marine life* in tons, rather than in numbers of individual animals:

> Fishing fleets dispose of 27 million tons of dead marine life each year. (C: 33)

In postmodern terms we could say that the animals are (mentally) *erased* through being named in collective terms (Olson 2000), a practice that may well be a precursor to their physical erasure.

Assumption 3: Humans Are at the Center of the World

The deep ecology movement recognizes that one of the root causes of ecological destruction is *anthropocentrism*, a form of human-centeredness that subordinates everything in nature to human concerns. Manes (1990: 142) writes that "The paradox of anthropocentrism is that a world conceived of only with human ends in mind seems destined to become inhospitable to any human ends in the long run." Some forms of environmentalism, and certainly the environmental education textbooks examined, rest upon an anthropocentric foundation through their use of terminology. The term *environment* itself is often used in ways that imply a separation between humans on one hand, and everything that surrounds them on the other (Cooper 2000: 1017).

Anthropocentric assumptions manifest themselves in many ways in the textbooks, particularly in descriptions of ecological damage that, although it impacts *all* life, is expressed only in terms of the impact on humans:

> Desertification . . . has had . . . a devastating effect on regional econo-
> mies and social conditions. (Y: 20)
>   As a result [of global warming] many coastal areas will be underwater
> and tens of millions of *people* will be made homeless. (V: 17, emphasis added)

In discussing pesticides and other agricultural chemicals, textbook A shows extreme human centeredness by considering the impact of the chemicals only on human health:

> Protecting the environment is often a difficult thing to do. That is why
> it is important to work out scientifically which chemicals are really dan-
> gerous to *humans*. (A: 21, emphasis added)

The implication of this sentence is that any chemical that does not harm humans is acceptable, no matter how much harm it may cause to other animals, plants, and the ecosystems on which human and all other life depends. A similar way of describing the effect of toxins is used in Textbook B:

> As these pollutants pass through the marine food chain, they are con-centrated in larger species, such as fish, which, when eaten, can poison *humans*. (B: 32, emphasis added)

No mention is made here of the possibility that the fish themselves may suffer from being poisoned. In fact, the idea that fish (or any other nonhuman animal) can feel pain because of environmental pollution is almost completely absent from the textbooks examined. As the example below from Textbook C illus-trates, pain is associated only with humans:

> Thousands of people ate contaminated fish from Minata Bay and died or became ill. They all suffered in great pain. (C: 33)

The order in which victims of ecological destruction are mentioned often reveals a hierarchy of their relative worth. For example, textbook Y states:

> If the necessary steps are not taken within the next 20 years, the North Sea fishing industry will probably be wiped out, along with many spe-cies of mammal. (Y: 9)

Here industry takes the direct position of *affected* in the passive construction, but the death of mammals appears only afterward, as a circumstantial adjunct. Furthermore, the death of mammals and the decline of industry are set up as *equivalents* (Fairclough 2003a: 88), since both are co-hyponyms of "wiped out entities." Fish, we might note, the primary victims of overfishing, are not men-tioned at all.

Textbook R gives a list of the "serious effects" of air pollution, starting with human health, mentioning forests at the end of the list, and completely failing to mention nonhuman animals:

> Air pollution has serious effects on human health, historical structures, masonry, brickwork, metal, sculptures and forests. (R: 27)

While the textbooks vary somewhat in the order they present victims, human welfare is always first, followed by human commercial interests, with animals and plants lower down in the list.

Often, the lives of other animals and plants are entirely overlooked. For example, textbook I states:

> The sea is vital in determining weather patterns of our world. The sea is an enormous source of food for mankind. The sea is also a source of minerals and especially oil that scientists can only dream of. Finally and not least, the sea is a great recreational resource for mankind. (I: 16)

Missing from this list is the fact that the sea is home for countless nonhuman animals; instead it is constructed as the equivalent of a human supermarket or playground. This leads to environmentalism that protects only places that have "wonderful wildlife" to entertain humans:

> Australia wants to keep the glorious colours and wonderful wildlife of its coral reef so that it can be enjoyed by its own citizens and the increasing numbers of visitors to Australia. (I: 17)

In the end, the aim of the environmental movement is reduced to that of preserving human pleasure, as expressed directly in the following example from textbook C:

> We must protect the world for ourselves and for future generations. Shouldn't our children be allowed the pleasures of clean air, natural forests, healthy food, and wild animals? (C: 3)

Assumption 4: Only Local People Are to Blame for Ecological Destruction
As mentioned before, the genre of shallow environmentalism tends to focus on immediate physical causes of ecological destruction, thereby placing responsibility only upon agents who are directly involved. The following examples illustrate this:

The main factors contributing to the process of desertification are the expansion of agricultural land, overgrazing, over-cultivation of poor soils and reckless deforestation. (R: 33)

Famine is caused by the following factors: 1) long spells of drought 2) population explosion 3) overtilling of cropland 4) poverty 5) deforestation and 6) civil war. (V: 69)

The expressions "overgrazing," "over-cultivation," "reckless deforestation," and "overtilling" are highly accusatory, yet the agents who are being accused have been diplomatically elided through nominalization. There are, however, a limited range of agents who graze and till and cultivate: local farmers are clear candidates, but the larger organizations that legitimize, encourage, or force their actions are not. The World Bank, the IMF, multinational corporations, or the international demand for cheap burger meat, for example, cannot take the position of the agent of "overtilling." Yet, as Stedman-Edwards (2001) points out, the explanation for destructive activities "is often found in socioeconomic forces that arise not at the local level but far from the sites of biodiversity loss."

Some textbooks are less diplomatic, explicitly identifying local people as the agents of material processes of destruction while ignoring other, more powerful actors:

The tropical rainforest in the Amazon Basin is being destroyed at a frightening pace, mainly because local people carry out slash-and-burn farming and partly because they fell trees for commercial purposes. (V: 5)

Another textbook, W, contains the patronizing presupposition that local people do not value their surroundings:

If local people can see people [ecotourists] coming from all corners of Earth to meet these animals and experience this forest, perhaps they will also find a new value in their surroundings (W: 48)

Textbook N makes the point that learning should be the other way round, with people from overdeveloped countries learning from indigenous people around the world about how to live sustainably. However, the textbook still manages to patronize indigenous peoples:

> They may be primitive according to our standards, but we have a great deal to learn from them. (N: 34)

As Smith and Williams (1999: 4) point out "One of the central problems with the culture associated with industrial growth societies is its lack of relationship to particular places and the way it is being imposed on the rest of the world." Rather than challenging this cultural imperialism, Textbook I seems to be encouraging it. In a chapter entitled "Creating a Global Culture," the textbook states:

> Some people are worried about the spread of a global culture; they fear that nations and peoples are losing their individuality. But the global culture is here to stay, so everyone might just as well relax, watch an American movie on television and eat a slice of pizza! (I: 77)

By setting up a dialogue with an imaginary interlocutor, this passage does bring in other voices, but the owners of those voices are only vaguely attributed to "some people." This allows the authors to frame arguments against current patterns of globalization in the way of their choosing, in this case as emotional reactions ("worried," "fear"). On the other hand, the categorical assertion "global culture is here to stay" is attributed to no one, thereby presenting it as an indisputable certainty.

DEEPER ECOLOGY WITHIN THE TEXTBOOKS

Although the discourse of the textbooks is overwhelmingly based on shallow environmentalism, there were occasional examples of deeper ecology, the most notable being Textbook U. This textbook gets to the root of ecological problems with examples like the following:

> The crash of the Exxon Valdez . . . was one of the worst oil spills in America's history . . . and the Exxon corporation spent an incredible

$2.2 billion trying to clean up the mess. . . . All of this money was duly recorded as contributing to the GNP of the United States. . . . Now imagine for a moment that the number of people who do volunteer work in the United States doubled. . . . All of these [volunteer] activities are productive and contribute to the quality of our life. . . . Yet none of them would be officially recorded as contributing to our nation since they are not calculated into our GNP. (U: 11)

The assumption that high GNP equals high quality of life is part of a hegemonic discourse that perpetuates a "misperception of its arbitrariness . . . so that it comes to be seen as transparently reflecting economic realities rather than constructing them in certain ways" (Chouliaraki and Fairclough 1999: 5). Examples like the one above challenge mainstream economic discourse by showing that "high GNP = high quality of life" is not a common sense assumption, but is, in fact, one of the myths at the root of the ecological crisis.

A very different example is the following from Textbook E, which uses the Gaia metaphor (the Earth is an organism) to set up an alternative discourse:

- In order to heal our own bodies we need to heal the Earth's body as well (E: 2)
- Unless we come to understand that the "body" of our earth—Gaia— is directly connected to our own body, we will not be serious about changing our habits to healthy ones. (E: 97)

These examples do not fully instantiate the Gaia metaphor, however, because saying that human bodies are "connected to" the Earth's body, rather than part of it, assumes that humans are separate from the Earth. This is similar to environmentalist assumptions that humans are separate from their surroundings (the environment).

The following examples also represent somewhat deeper ecological ideas, by encouraging empathy with nonhuman life:

- Thousands of trees and animals have died, and forest people have lost their homes, so that today North Americans can eat cheap meat. (S: 15)

· Even with safety measures, approximately 155,000 sea turtles drown
  in shrimp nets each year. (G: 13)

The first quote puts the nonhuman individuals who suffer from ecological destruction first, using the word "die" for both animals and trees, rather than euphemisms such as "wiped out" (Y: 9). The second example encourages empathy
by mentioning the type of animals who suffer by name (sea turtles), highlighting their individuality by enumerating them (155,000 sea turtles), and explicitly
mentioning their cause of death (drown). This is in stark contrast to Textbook
K's rendition of the same situation: "Millions of tons of . . . 'by-catch' . . . are
thrown overboard" (K: 26).

Overall, however, there are very few examples of the discourse of deep ecology within the textbooks. With the exception of Textbook U, the cultural practices that lie at the root of ecological destruction remain virtually unchallenged,
and no alternative vision is proposed.

ECOLOGICAL INSIGHT WITHIN JAPANESE CULTURE

At the heart of traditional Japanese culture is a form of ecology far deeper than
the shallow environmentalism of the textbooks. This ecological awareness is
based on Buddhist ideals of compassion and Taoist ideals of flowing with nature,
as they converge in Zen and become manifest in poetry, calligraphy, pottery,
and other cultural practices. Ecological insight, in the sense it is used here, consists of awareness of relationships between humans, animals, and plants as part
of the larger life processes that allow all living beings to thrive.

That is not to say that all strands of traditional Japanese culture are compatible with humane treatment of animals and ecological sustainability. The rigid
hierarchy of Confucianism places humans above all other animals (Stone 1999),
and some forms of Buddhism display "what westerners would see as quite cruel
behaviour to animals . . . based on the available notion of reincarnation in an
animal, female, or deformed body as punishment for past imperfections" (Haraway 1989: 247). Some ways of expressing compassion, too, do not necessarily

imply the "biocentric equality" of deep ecology, but rather construe "relation-ships to animals, women or other suffering beings in ways similar to masculinist human stewardship . . . [which] insist on dominance and subordination within a social and ontological unity" (Haraway 1989: 247).

These hierarchical tendencies may have contributed to Japan's becoming one of the most ecologically destructive countries on Earth. Other factors in-clude consumerist ideologies imported from the West, the headlong rush toward economic supremacy, the deeply rooted cultural desire to be in control, and the inability to appraise and stop a course of action once it has been started (Kerr 2002). The deep ecological sensitivity of Zen, therefore, must not be seen as a representation of all Japanese culture, but rather a reaction against the more hierarchical and destructive elements that coexist within it. Although it is nec-essary to be selective, aspects of traditional Japanese culture can be drawn on as a source of inspiration for ways of interacting more sustainably with natural systems. The following are examples of such aspects.

Each time Japanese people sit down to eat, they perform a ritual with eco-logical implications: the recitation of the word *itadakimasu*. Literally the polite form of the word "receive," *itadakimasu* expresses thanks for the lives of the animals and plants who died for the food, and those who worked to prepare the food. *Itadakimasu* is just one aspect of *naikan* (Krech 2002): consciousness of, and regret for, disturbing others, whether those others happen to be people, other animals, plants, rivers, or mountains. *Naikan* as a cultural value, in contrast to consumerism, encourages the use of the minimum necessary resources with gratitude and appreciation.

Material simplicity is not considered a sacrifice, but instead appreciated as a realization of the cultural ideal of *Wabi*: "to be poor, that is, not to be dependent on things worldly — wealth, power, and reputation — and yet to feel inwardly the presence of something of the highest value" (Suzuki 1970: 23). The aesthetic of *wabi* permeates traditional Japanese arts, for example in the design of rooms used for the tea ceremony:

> The tea room . . . does not pretend to be other than a mere cottage—a
> straw hut as we call it. . . . The materials used in its construction are in-

tended to give the suggestion of refined poverty. Yet we must remember that all this is the result of profound artistic forethought. (Okakura 1956: 54)

Within the discourse that is used during the tea ceremony, conversation is limited to admiration of the tea bowls and implements, the seasonal scroll hanging in the alcove, the flower in a vase below the scroll, the view outside the tea room and other things that are immediately present in sensual reality. The tea ceremony is not a place for abstract arguing about politics; instead, it is a space for reconnection with the reality of other people and nature.

In line with *naikan*, the discourse of a particularly important genre of haiku poems shows respect toward other animals and nature, as reflected in the following poem by Uejima Onitsura:

gyōzui no / sutedokoro naki / mushi no koe
no place / to throw out the bathwater / sound of insects
(in Bowers 1996: 38)

Understanding the meaning of this haiku requires two *bridging assumptions*: (a) that the insects are in the place that Onitsura usually throws his bathwater, and (b) that it would be unthinkable to harm them by pouring bathwater on them. Bridging assumptions that place a high value on all life are central to the discourse of haiku, and counter any tendency toward human-centeredness.

In haiku, rather than valuing others for their rarity or usefulness, appreciation is expressed for the ordinary plants, birds, insects and other animals that people interact with everyday. This encourages a form of direct ecological consciousness that is not mediated by museums, zoos or abstractions such as the totalizing term "environment." As Suzuki points out, nature is considered as a "constant friend and companion" (1970: 334), rather than a force to be conquered.

Within Japanese culture, even modern Japanese culture, there is a great fondness for the seasons and the natural cycles they represent. All haiku contain a word connoting the season, and many festivals revolve around the viewing of seasonal phenomena: the cherry blossoms, seasonal flowers, autumn leaves, and fireflies. Seasonal food is highly prized, and Japanese people have traditionally looked forward to *matsutake* mushrooms in autumn, *mikan* (mandarin oranges) in winter, watermelon in summer, and bamboo shoots in spring. This leads to the ecological practice of eating locally grown fresh fruits and vegetables in season. With *naikan* ensuring that animal products are kept to a minimum, and *wabi* ensuring that portions are small and unrefined, the result is one of the healthiest and most ecologically beneficial diets in the world.

In traditional Japanese arts and crafts, it is simplicity and closeness to nature that are prized: tea bowls are rough and irregular-shaped and show off the natural texture of the clay; whisks are cut from a single piece of bamboo; houses are built and decorated with local, natural materials. Perfect geometric shapes, monochrome colors, and symmetry are disdained as unnecessarily repetitive and unnatural (Okakura 1956: 54). Respect for nature is manifest not only in haiku, but in the objects that surround people in their everyday lives. A practical ecological benefit of this is that crafts are made by hand using the minimum necessary materials gathered locally, and the localization of craft is still important in Japan, each region having its own highly prized specialities (*meibutsu*).

Naikan, *wabi*, the love of nature, and traditional craftsmanship are all manifestations of Zen, Buddhist, and Taoist traditions that lie at the heart of traditional Japanese culture. These traditions address the deep psychological split that has occurred between human thinking and nature, the split that eco-psychologists claim is at the heart of ecological destruction (see Kanner, Roszak, and Gomes 1995). For example, in discussing intellectual abstraction and the separation of subject and object, Suzuki (1970: 359) writes:

> There has never been any separation between subject and object, and all the discrimination and separation we have or, rather, make is a later creation. . . . The aim of Zen is thus to restore the experience of original inseparability.

Zen arts and meditative practices offer a range of ways to put artificial intellectual discriminations into perspective (Harada 1993) and pay attention to the "multiple levels of connection" (Conn 1995: 159) that are at the heart of all ecological systems.

Consideration of Japanese ecological ideas shows, at the very least, that ecologically destructive "commonsense" assumptions in the West are contingent, and that alternatives are available. At best, the alternative constructions of Japanese ecology have the potential to address some of the deep cultural causes of ecological destruction that are ignored, or even entrenched, by shallow environmentalism.

Smith and Williams (1999: 3) argue that in the United States "classes in environmental education focus on scientific analysis and social policy," and "missing in most of these efforts is a recognition of the deeper cultural transformations that must accompany the shift to more ecologically sustainable ways of life" (33). This chapter has shown how English-language environmental textbooks spread this form of shallow environmental education abroad, in this case, to Japan.

It is important to question why the textbooks fail to challenge those Western cultural values implicated in ecological destruction. One explanation may be that spreading consumerist ideology, along with flattering portraits of the West, is a standard way of opening up overseas markets, and English-language teaching has been, and remains, deeply implicated in this process (Phillipson 1992, Pennycook 1998).

However, despite the influence of cultural imperialism, traditional values in Japan have not been lost entirely, and Japanese students still have access to many aspects of their culture. Nearly all students have visited Japanese-style houses, have eaten traditional Japanese food, have gone on *hanami* picnics to view cherry blossoms, have heard lyrics about seasons and nature in *enka* music, have said *itadakimasu* before eating, and many have taken part in tea ceremonies, *ikebana* flower arranging classes, and calligraphy classes.

Traditional culture may not be a top priority for young people in Japan, but it only takes a small stimulus for them to remember traditional values and consider their application to the ecological problems of the modern world. For example, sixty students in a university English class in Fukuoka were asked to consult with elders and write an essay entitled "Why Do Japanese People Say *Itadakimasu*?" The students responded with great enthusiasm, and their answers showed not only a clear understanding of, but also pride in, traditional Japanese values. The following extracts from the essays were typical:

- My grandmother said [*itadakimasu*] expresses gratitude to the plants and animals that were enjoying life before being killed by humans. My mother says we say *itadakimasu* to thank the people who prepare and grow the food. Finally my friend says she thinks nothing when she says *itadakimasu*.
- *Itadakimasu* means I'll receive your life as my life. . . . We think of all living things, all plants and animals, as having precious lives.
- Many animals become our victims. They probably wanted to be alive for a long time enjoying the world, but we took everything they had from them. Saying *itadakimasu* is a way of expressing gratitude to the animals.
- Plants and animals don't exist for people to eat them.
- Through *itadakimasu* we learn about the connection of life.
- [Saying *itadakimasu*] is a wonderful part of Japanese culture.

Some students also connected *itadakimasu* to the ecological principle of not wasting or overconsuming:

- I work in a food store. There is always a lot of left over wasted food. This is very impolite to the animals and plants who have died for our dinner.
- It is impolite to living things to be fussy [about what we eat]. We must not waste leftover food.

Similarly, when students wrote about the architecture and decoration of Japanese-style houses, the tea ceremony, and traditional Japanese food, they showed a deep appreciation of traditional Japanese values, and could see their relevance to the modern ecological crisis. Traditional Japanese culture, then, is one possible source of alternative discourses that are based on quite different assumptions from those that underpin modern unsustainable cultures. The following two chapters investigate discourses from traditional Japanese culture in detail, exploring their potential for providing alternative ways of representing animals and nature.

TABLE 7.1 **Environmental Education Textbooks**

Textbook A	Andrew Bennetto and Heather Jones. *Protecting the Environment*. Tokyo: Macmillan Language House, 2000.
Textbook B	Paul Allum. *Our Planet, Our Future*. Tokyo: Seibido, 1994.
Textbook C	Greg Goodmacher. *Nature and the Environment*. Seibido, 1999.
Textbook D	David Peaty. *You, Me, and the World*. Tokyo: Kinseido, 1997.
Textbook E	Bruce Allen. *Environment and Health*. Tokyo: Seibido, 2000.
Textbook F	JoAnn Parochetti, Tsuyoshi Chiba, Junko Yoshino, and Akio Homma. *Bountiful Economics*. Tokyo: Nan'un-do, 2001.
Textbook G	Yukio Seya, Masahiro Takatsu, Seiko Hirai, and David Brooks. *Beyond Tomorrow: Science Looks at the Future*. Tokyo: Nan'un-do, 1998.
Textbook H	Shane Novak and Masakazu Someya. *Read the Sea*. Tokyo: Sanshusha, 1996.
Textbook I	John Randle, Lisa Gerard-Sharp, and Yasuo Yagi. *Global Issues Today*. Tokyo: Seibido, 1997
Textbook J	Bernadette Vallely. *66 Ways to Save the Earth*. Tokyo: Nan'un-do, 1991.
Textbook K	Richard Evanoff, Charles Paxton, and Hugh Paxton. *Make It or Break It: The Future of Our Environment*. Tokyo: Sanshusha, 1999.
Textbook L	Paul Allum, *Save Our Planet*. Tokyo: Seibido, 1995.
Textbook M	David Peaty. *Global Challenges*. Tokyo: Kinseido, 1990.
Textbook N	David Peaty. *Global Perspectives*. Tokyo: Kinseido, 1995.
Textbook O	Jo Potter and Andy Hopkins. *Animals in Danger*. Oxford: Oxford University Press, 1996.
Textbook P	Masatoshi Tabuki and Robert Long. *Critical Insight on Contemporary Issues*. Tokyo: Seibido, 2001.
Textbook Q	John Lander. *Another Green World*. Tokyo: Kinseido, 1993.
Textbook R	1997 Saburo Yamamura and Kenneth Macdonald. *Planet Problems*. Tokyo: Seibido
Textbook S	Rowena Akinyemi. *Rainforests*. Oxford: Oxford University Press, 1995.
Textbook T	John Janovy. *Ten Minute Ecologist*. Tokyo: Kinseido, 1997.
Textbook U	Richard Evanoff. *Thinking about the Environment: An Introduction to Environmental Ethics*. Tokyo: Macmillan Language House, 1996.
Textbook V	Yamaura Saburo and K Macdonald. *Wake Up World*. Tokyo: Kinseido, 1992.
Textbook W	Kazuya Asakawa, Chisa Uetsuki, Caitlin Stronell, Beverley Lafaye. *Taking Action on Global Issues*. Tokyo: Sanshusha, 2002.
Textbook X	Jim Knudsen and Takao Maruyama. *Saving Our Planet*. Tokyo: Nan'un-do, 1993.
Textbook Y	David Peaty *Environmental Issues*. Tokyo: Macmillan Language House, 1995.
Textbook Z	Paul Allum. *Progress in Our World: Technology, the Environment and Society*. Tokyo: Seibido, 2000.

8

Haiku and Beyond

This chapter takes a closer look at the discourse of haiku as one based on very different assumptions from both those of destructive discourses and counter-discourses in the West. The starting point is with the origins of human separation from animals and the natural world, and this leads on to a discussion of how haiku can facilitate reconnection.

In *The Spell of the Sensuous*, David Abram (1996) locates the start of the ever increasing separation between humans and the rest of nature in the invention of writing systems. No longer was language something fine-tuned to the community and land in a particular region, instead it became quite literally disembodied, cut free from the writer, and able to spread itself to new domains. Traditional stories about the local animals, plants, rivers, and trees became swamped by writing from different bioregions and different times. In addition, writing facilitates "sparsely linear or analytic thought" (Ong 2002: 40), resulting in "analytic categories that depend on writing to structure knowledge at a distance from lived experience" (Ong 2002: 42).

In countries where writing is preeminent, the relationship between humans and other life-forms is increasingly mediated by language and other media. It is becoming more likely for people to come across animals and plants as they are represented in books, magazines, advertisements, films, toys, and clip-art than to notice them face-to-face in everyday life. There is growing awareness, particularly when it comes to the relationship between humans and other animals, of the importance of linguistic mediation, and the significant effects this can have (Glenn 2004, Schillo 2003, Dunayer 2001, Scarce 2000, Kheel 1995).

From these studies a picture is emerging of a wide range of discourses that construct relationships with animals in ways that further the separation between humans and the rest of nature. As discussed earlier, there is the jocular way that animals are used as insults in everyday conversation (chapters 1 and 2, also Goatly 2006), the more sinister way that animals are objectified and treated as inconsequential by the discourse of the meat industry (chapters 1 and 2, also Dunayer 2001), and the way that animals are treated separately from humans as part of the "environment" by environmentalist discourse (chapter 7). In addition, ecological discourse often treats animals and the ecosystems they are part of as resources for human use; conservationist discourse tends to treat animals as mattering only if they belong to a rare charismatic species; and finally, animal rights discourses represent animals narrowly as passive victims rather than agents of their own lives (chapter 4).

Most studies of the discursive representation of nature have focused on discourses that have the potential to create undesirable relationships between humans and other life-forms—relationships of exploitation that lead not only to the suffering of animals, but also to ecological damage and negative impacts on humans. While critical awareness of dominant discourses and their potentially damaging effects is important, the next stage is analysis of alternative discourses that have the potential to construct more harmonious relationships between humans and the more-than-human world.

Abram (1996), Snyder (2000), and Bate (2000) all agree that if people have lost touch with the natural world around them, and are engrossed in a symbolic world of writing, then it is through this symbolic world that people need to be reached initially and encouraged to enter into new relationships with the more-than-human world. Abram (1996) puts this eloquently, in a writing style consistent with its message:

> There can be no question of simply abandoning literacy, of turning away from all writing. Our task, rather, is that of *taking up* the written word, with all of its potency, and patiently, carefully, writing language back into the land. Our craft is that of releasing the budded, earthy intelli-

gence of our words, freeing them to respond to the speech of the things themselves—to the green uttering-forth of leaves from the spring branches. (Abram 1996: 273)

But how can writers write language back into the land in ways that contribute to more harmonious relationships between humans and the other animals, plants, and soil that make up that land? Answering this question requires a journey beyond mainstream Western discourses such as those of industry, biological science, and even environmentalism or ecology: a journey to discover new ways of representing the more-than-human world that break free of the assumptions of dominant Western discourses. In particular, it is important to discover discourses that overcome the assumption that other animals and plants are objects, human possessions, individually inconsequential tokens of species, or that their value lies only in their rarity or short-term utility to humans.

There are many places we can look for alternative discourses, from English Romantic poets (Bate 2000, Goatly 2000) to traditional cultures around the world that express a particular intimacy with, and embeddedness in, the natural world. This chapter explores the discourse of traditional Japanese *haiku*, analyzing the assumptions it is based on, and the way that it represents relationships between humans and other forms of life.

Although the chapter refers to "*the* discourse of haiku" it is important that a discussion of haiku does not propose that there is an "essence" of haiku running through every example. The "discourse of haiku" analyzed here exists in patterns that run through large numbers of haiku, though by no means all. The patterns come about partly through convention, but also through revolutions caused by great masters, who rejected the style of haiku that came before, gave new directions to the discourse, and provided key examples that many others emulated. There are therefore a large number of discourses within the genre of *haiku*, and what is described here is just one of these. It is, however, one that can be considered highly significant, both in terms of cultural impact and ecological wisdom.

To discover the patterns that make up the discourse of haiku, a corpus of several thousand haiku was gathered from ten anthologies (Addiss, Yamamoto, and Yamamoto 1996, 1992, Aitken 1978, Bowers 1996, Blyth 1995, Henderson 1958, Higginson 1996, Mackenzie 1957, Miura 1991, Ueda 2003), and one online collection (Lanoue 2006). These haiku are very much "classic," coming from the period between 1682 (when Bashō revolutionised haiku with his "frog" poem), to 1902, the date when the last of the four great masters, Shiki, died. The haiku of these four masters (Bashō, Issa, Buson, and Shiki) form a sizeable part of the corpus because of their profound influence, though other poets who follow a similar style are also included.

The following sections describe seven aspects of haiku that represent relationships between humans and the more-than-human world in ways very different from dominant mainstream discourses in the West.

APPRECIATION OF THE ORDINARY

> tsukubōte / kumo wo ukagau / kaeru kana
>
> crouching / peering up at the clouds / a frog
>
> (Chiyo, in Addiss et al. 1992: 92)

Rather than valuing others for their rarity, size, charisma, or usefulness, haiku express appreciation for the ordinary plants, birds, insects, and animals that people interact with in daily life. Suzuki (1970: 263) describes how Bashō wrote haiku on the *nazuna* herb, a plant that is "humble . . . not at all pretty and charming":

> yoku mireba / nazuna hana saku / kakine kana
>
> when closely inspected / the *nazuna* is flowering / by the hedge
>
> (in Suzuki 1970: 263)

Similarly, in discussing another of Bashō's haiku about buckwheat flowers (below), Ueda (1982: 66) points out that "buckwheat flowers are commonplace in Japan and not especially beautiful; moreover, buckwheat is the main ingredient of one of the plainest foods, noodles."

mikazuki ni / chi wa oboro nari / soba no hana

under the crescent moon / the earth looms hazily— / buckwheat flowers

(in Ueda 1982: 66)

Bashō's sense of appreciation for the *nazuna* and buckwheat flowers is not explicit in these haiku—he does not refer to "the beauty of the buckwheat flowers," for instance. However, deep appreciation can be inferred because of the nature of the discourse of haiku itself. There are so many haiku that describe culturally appreciated aspects of nature (such as cherry blossoms or fireflies) that the assumption "the subject highlighted by the haiku is to be treated with appreciation" is built into the discourse, a taken-for-granted background assumption that does not need to be stated. By placing the buckwheat flowers within the same frame as is frequently used for cherry blossoms, Bashō is implicitly stating that they too are worthy of similar appreciation.

Like Bashō, Issa writes only about common, local animals and plants, a fact that can be confirmed by searching through Lanoue's (2006) impressive collection of 7,000 of Issa's poems. Within this collection there are no poems about lions, tigers, elephants, or pandas. Instead, there are haiku about a huge variety of common animals and plants of the kind people in Japan were likely to come across in their everyday lives. The following list shows some of the animals appearing in Issa's haiku:

A butterfly, cuckoo, dog, dragonfly, duck, geese, flea, frog, mouse, mosquito, nightingale, snake, sparrow, swallow, snail, toad, lice, fly, skylark, sparrow, cat, horsefly, puppy, pigeon, crow, deer, titmouse, earthworms, lark, cicada, frog, crab, monkey, fox, silkworm, chicken, pheasant, thrush, horse, wren, fawn, nightingale, ant, turtle, snipe, blowfish, pony, wren, pheasant, winnow, stork, spider, crane, locusts, kitten, cormorant, shrike, rooster.

Despite the large number of animals and plants named in Issa's 7,000 haiku, abstract category names above the species level rarely appear, except in the case of *tori* (bird) and *mushi* (insect). So we do not find any instances of the words *dōbutsu* (animal), *ikimono* or *seibutsu* (living thing), *shokubutsu* (plant), *ueki* (cultivated plant), *honyūrui* (mammal), or *hachūrui* (reptile). This is because haiku record and encourage encounters with real animals and plants, rather than engage in rational discussion of abstract categories.

The focus on the actual and the everyday is important because it encourages direct encounters with living animals and plants in natural settings rather than encounters mediated by museums, zoos or linguistic abstractions. Haiku therefore have the potential to contribute to ecological consciousness tuned to the local environment, where careful observation of the way things are in nature is combined with a sense of value and appreciation.

Despite the brevity of haiku, the individual animals and plants that are encountered are never described in isolation from their immediate environment. The linking of the particular animals and plants with their wider context is carried out through a season word (*kigo*). Kigo are an essential part of the discourse of haiku, placing each haiku in a particular season, and thereby allowing the reader's imagination to fill in missing details of the surroundings. In the haiku that started this section, the season word *kaeru* (frog) represents spring, which is when frogs make themselves most noticeable through their croaking.

Haiku, by their very existence, demonstrate recognition of special worth in the subjects they describe—enough worth to stimulate the poet to carefully craft a poem about them consisting of exactly seventeen syllables (three lines of five, seven, and five syllables respectively). This structure gives poets a chance to give special emphasis to the plant or animal through dedicating all five syllables of either the first or last line to their name. Both these positions are important because the first line is the *Theme* of the haiku and the last line provides end-focus. For instance:

> hototogisu / ware mo kiai no / yoki hi nari
>
> cuckoo— / today I'm in good spirits / too
>
> (Issa in Lanoue 2006)

In this haiku, the whole first line is the name of a species of bird, *hototogisu* (a Japanese cuckoo), which conveniently has five syllables. Where names have fewer than five syllables, pivot words (*kakekotoba*) such as *ya* or *kana* are inserted, which add further poetic emphasis. Pivot words cannot be translated into English, though translators sometimes use the expressions "ah!" or "oh!"—for example, *suzume-go ya* (ah! baby sparrow) or *kaeru kana* (oh! frog). The addition of a pivot word shows clearly and strongly that the haiku is dedicated to the plant or animal.

By taking ordinary animals and plants, and giving them a prime position within a highly appreciated cultural art form, haiku give the message that they are important for themselves, with no need for recourse to abstractions such as the "intrinsic value of nature" used in the discourse of deep ecology.

ANIMALS AND PLANTS AS AGENTS AND SENSERS

The overwhelming majority of animals and plants that are represented in haiku are not doing anything unusual or having anything done to them by humans, but are doing what they would normally do:

> ki wo ochite / hebi no chi wo hau / atsusa kana
>
> falling from a tree / the snake slithers on the ground / in this heat
>
> (Shikyu, in Addiss et al. 1992: 88)

> aoyagi ni / kōmori tsutau / yūbaeya
>
> a bat flies / along the rows of green willows / in the evening glow (Kikaku, in Addiss et al. 1992: 29)

> yudachi ya / kusaba wo tsukamu / mura suzume
>
> caught in a sudden shower / huddling sparrows / vie to get at the grass leaves
>
> (Buson, in Miura 1991: 45)

A closer look at the thematic roles that animals take in clauses helps to reveal the linguistic techniques that haiku use to represent animals as leading their own lives. Taking an illustrative sample of thirty-six haiku selected from several of the collections, we find that the most common role is that of *agent* of material processes. By giving animals and plants agentive roles, the poets represent them as actively involved in leading their own lives for their own purposes: bees buzz, clover blooms, ants crawl, insects sing, and so on. Among the thirty-six illustrative haiku there are thirteen cases of material processes, which can be represented as follows:

> Material process (*agent*): buzzes (bee), blooms (clover), sprouts (wild-flower), crawls (ant), stretches (crane), rises (horse), sings (insect), feast (mosquitoes), take baths (monkeys), flits (butterfly), searches (cat), sings (bird), flies (crane).

The second most common role that animals (and in one case a tree) play is as the *senser* in mental processes—frogs peer, fish know, birds envy, and so on. Of the thirty-six haiku there are nine mental processes, as follows:

> Mental process (*senser*): peers (frog), know (fish), know (ant), envy (bird), know (bird), know (hornet), like (dragonfly), is grateful (tree), waits (sparrow).

The third most frequent role that animals and plants play is as *addressee* in clauses, where the author speaks directly to the animal or plant:

> kirigirisu / koe wo karasu na / asu mo aki
>
> katydid! / don't get hoarse / tomorrow is autumn too
>
> (Issa, in Lanoue 2006)

Within the selection, haiku are directly addressed to eight different kinds of animal and one kind of plant:

> (*Addressee*): geese, katydids, a frog, spiders, a crab, flees, chrysanthe-mums, a cuckoo.

A rarer role that plants and animals find themselves in is as the *affected* partici-pant in material processes. There are four cases of this: violets are the *affected* participant of the process of being picked, chrysanthemums have washing water thrown all over them, roses are cut, and a heron is shot.

Material process (*affected*): picking (violets), splashing (chrysanthemums), cutting (rose), shooting (heron)

The *affected* role is a common place that animals and plants are found in dominant discourses of the West — animals and plants are represented as passively
affected by human actions rather than as capable of action themselves. These
haiku representations are slightly different, however, in that each demonstrates a degree of sympathy for the suffering of the plant/animal at human
hands:

> nanigoto ka / bara ni tsubuyaki / bara wo kiru
>
> whispering / something to the rose / she cuts the rose
>
> (Kuroda, in Ueda 2003: 203)

> tsumu mo oshi / tsumanu mo oshiki / sumire kana
>
> I regret picking / and not picking / violets
>
> (Anonymous, in Bowers 1996: 36)

Finally, in two cases, animals are de-emphasized through being embedded in
noun phrases: *semi no koe* (voice of the cicada), and *mushi no koe* (voice of insects).
Like the *affected* role, embeddedness is frequently used in mainstream Western
discourses with the result of representing animals at a distance. In these two
haiku, however, the distance may reflect the actual indirectness of relationships
with insects that can be heard but not seen.

In general then, clause structure in haiku represents animals and plants as
beings who are actively involved in leading their own lives in ways consistent
with their nature, whether that is flying, slithering, or blooming. They represent animals in particular as beings with mental lives, who know, feel, and
have desires. Both animals and plants are offered the recognition of being living beings directly addressable by humans, and in the rare cases where plants/
animals are represented as the objects of human interference, there is a degree
of sympathy implied.

All of this would be unremarkable — just representations of the way things
are in nature — if it were not for the power of dominant discourses in the West

to represent animals and plants very differently: as objects, machines, substances, or variables in financial equations.

THINGS THE WAY THEY ARE: *SONOMAMA*

The vast majority of verbs in haiku are in the plain dictionary form, corresponding most closely with the straight present tense in English. The verbs "slither" (*hau*), "fly/swing" (*tsutau*), "grab" (*tsukamu*), "dry out" (*karasu*), and "cut" (*kiru*) in the previous section were all in this form. Another form, *keri*, appears in Haiku, though far less frequently. *Keri* was originally a past tense marker in classical Japanese, but is also used to give poetic emphasis to events in the present. In general, then, haiku represent an appreciation of the present moment rather than a reconstructed narrative or story of something that happened in the past.

The appreciation of the ordinary, the direct encounter with animals and plants that happen to be around, the way these plants and animals are being themselves, and, crucially, the emphasis on the present moment, link haiku with the Buddhist ideal of suchness (*tathata*), or *sonomama* in colloquial Japanese (Suzuki 1970: 230). *Sonomama* is just the way that things are, unsullied by conceptualizations or abstractions that attempt to make them something they are not. If the discourses of the meat industry, environmentalism, and animal rights in the West represent animals and plants in ways that erase their true nature, then haiku is an attempt to erase that nature as little as possible. Haiku can express the concept of *sonomama* in ways that would be impossible in prose, as the following haiku about the most ordinary patrinia flower (*ominaeshi*) illustrates:

ominaeshi / sono kuki nagara / hana nagara

the ominaeshi / the stems as they are / the flowers as they are

(Bashō in Bowers 1996: 18)

In the context of the appreciation of the ordinary that is built into the discourse of haiku, this haiku shows appreciation for the suchness of the ominaeshi in their natural state. The appreciation of *sonomama* is not just aesthetic appreciation, but extends to nonviolent action too, as expressed by Chiyo in a haiku that was mentioned in the previous chapter:

asagao ni / tsurube torarete / moraimizu

morning glory! / the well-bucket entangled / I ask for water

(in Bowers 1996: 44)

The final "te" of *torarete* connects the second and third lines, indicating that the reason for borrowing water has something to do with the fact that the well bucket has been entangled by the flower. There is a semantic "gap" between these two situations (the well-bucket being entangled and asking for water)—how are they related? The gap is filled by a background assumption existing in the discourse of haiku that nature needs to be respected and not disturbed unnecessarily. The meaning of this haiku, then, if we had to write it in full in prose, is: "Having left her house one autumn morning to draw water, Chiyo arrived at her well to find a morning-glory, a common flower, wrapped around the well bucket. Showing a deep respect and appreciation, she refrained from disturbing it, borrowing water from a neighbor's well instead." This illustrates that when haiku are read in the context of the discourse they belong to, a much larger meaning can be extracted from their brief seventeen syllables.

The importance of *sonomama* in an age of genetic engineering is clear, and well expressed by Chuang Tzu, writing in the fourth century BCE from a Taoist perspective, Taoism having a major influence on haiku:

Every addition to or deviation to nature belongs not to the ultimate perfection . . . for . . . a duck's legs, though short, cannot be lengthened without pain to the duck, and a crane's legs, though long, cannot be shortened without misery to the crane (Chuang Tzu 2001: 57)

THE AVOIDANCE OF METAPHOR

yase-gaeru / makeru na Issa / kore ni ari

lean frog / don't you surrender! / here's Issa by you

(Mackenzie 1957: 12)

Mackenzie (1957) and Lanoue (2006) contextualize the above poem in two very different ways. Mackenzie claims it refers to when "Issa looked down on an uneven duel in Musashi, that home of swordsmen," which would make this haiku a metaphor where the frog stands for a human. On the other hand, Lanoue's explanation is quite different:

> In his diary, Issa explains, "I stooped to watch a frog scuffle on the 20th day of Fourth Month." Evidently, he did not remain an impartial observer, but plunged into the fray to help out a scrawny frog. (Lanoue 2006)

In Lanoue's version, it is really a frog that Issa saw. This explanation is more likely, because central to the discourse of haiku is the ideal of a poet who "presents an observation of a natural, often commonplace event, in plainest diction, without verbal trickery" (Stryk 1985: 12). It would severely disrupt the imagery of haiku if every time we read a haiku we had to decide whether to imagine the actual animals or plants or think of some indirect reference to the human world. Britton (1974: 10) and Ooka (1997: 103) both describe how in haiku nothing is contrived, and with each word only having one meaning, there is no need to seek for hidden references. In this way, the discourse of haiku emphasizes the importance of the animals and plants in themselves rather than simply using them as metaphors for the human world.

However, there are, in fact, haiku that contain obvious metaphors, and this is because haiku are created for a wide variety of communicative purposes, including thanking a guest or bidding farewell, and not all record moments of identification with nature. Haiku have even been used for asking for a divorce:

hechima tsuru / kitte shimaeba / moto no mizu

if you've severed it / the vine of the gourd plant / throw it back in the water

(Issa in Mackenzie 1957: 45)

This is Issa, writing to his wife after she left him to live with her father. While acknowledging that such haiku exist, they are of little interest here, and are often described as not being true haiku, for instance by Shiki, who insists that haiku should involve "drawing from nature" (*shasei*), rather than relying on metaphor and symbol. As Bashō explains "Go to the pine if you want to learn about the pine, or to the bamboo if you want to learn about the bamboo." (in Yuasa 1967: 33).

IDENTITY

Without being symbolic or metaphorical, haiku do often reveal the identity, on certain planes, of humans and other forms of life. As Lanoue (2006) points out, Issa in the frog haiku above identifies with the frog; "because he likes to describe himself as impoverished and hungry, Issa feels a special kinship with the scrawny frog." Issa could see himself in the frog, something that could be considered a dissolution of subject and object of the kind that Bashō describes: "Your poetry issues of its own accord when you and the object have become one — when you have plunged deep enough into the object to see something like a hidden glimmering there" (in Yuasa 1967). This dissolution can be seen in many haiku, especially those about cherry blossoms and other transient natural phenomena:

saku hana ya / kono yo-zumai mo / ima sukoshi

cherry blossoms— / residents of this world, too / a short time

(Issa, in Lanoue 2006)

It is evident from the particle *mo*, meaning "too" that this is *not* a metaphor of cherry blossoms symbolizing the transient nature of human life. Instead, the cherry blossom and the human are both manifestations of the same cycle of life from birth to death, which is transient in one as it is in the other. This goes beyond simile to a literal comparison, which expresses the realization of identity within a particular plane, in this case the plane of being alive.

The particle *mo* is frequently used to reveal identity with all kinds of life, for example, between the poet and a dragonfly, both enjoying the evening, or to a bedraggled monkey, or even a butterfly:

akatonbo / kare mo yūbe ga / suki ja yara

red dragonfly / he's one too that likes the evening / or so it seems (Issa in Mackenzie 1957: 65)

hatsu shigure / saru mo komino wo / hoshige nari

first winter rain / the monkey also seems to wish / for a little straw cloak

(Bashō, in Suzuki 1970: 232)

chō tonde / wagami mo chiri no / tagui kana

butterfly flitting— / I too am made / of dust

(Lanoue 2006)

The sense of identity expressed in haiku accords closely with Chang Tsu's Taoist concept of identity:

> Only the truly intelligent understand this principle of the identity of all things. They do not view things as apprehended by themselves . . . but transfer themselves into the position of the things viewed. . . . And viewing them thus they are able to comprehend them. (Chuang Tzu 2001: 23)

Ooka (1997: 109) subtly points out the benefits of this kind of identification with nature, as opposed to Western viewpoints. In his words, Japanese classical poets "were unable to establish a clear distinction between self and other, to discover in their dissimilarity to others the foundation of their own individuality, and to consider rivalry and confrontation as something altogether natural."

EMPATHY, UNCONDITIONAL POSITIVE REGARD, CONGRUENCE

Empathy is similar to identity, but rather than noticing a commonality of experience, empathy requires imaginatively projecting oneself into the different perspective and emotions of another. Empathy is sometimes signalled with the particle *ni* (to the):

hanaabu ni / kabocha no hana no / naka nukuki

to the drone fly / the pumpkin flower's inside / is snug

(Tsuji, in Ueda 2003: 214)

This shows the ability to imagine the world from another's point of view, as do the following, which use a variety of linguistic techniques:

uo domoya / oke to mo shirade / kadosuzumi

the fish / don't know they're in a bucket— / cooling by the gate

(Issa, in Addiss et al. 1992: 96)

asamashi to / fugu ya miruran / hito no kao

maybe pitiful / to the blowfish . . . / people's faces

(Issa, in Lanoue 2006)

warera gi wa / tada yakamashii / hototogisu

our ceremony— / just a lot of noise / to the cuckoo

(Issa, in Lanoue 2006)

Where empathy is for the suffering of others, it is synonymous with compassion, and haiku show a great deal of compassion. It is worth giving several examples of this because of its central place in the discourse of haiku:

fuyu bachi no / shini dokoro naku / aruki keri

a winter bee / no place to die / walking along

(Kijo, in Miura 1991: 101, translation adapted)

no wa kareru / nobasu mono nashi / tsuru no kubi

in the withered fields / there's no need for the crane / to stretch out its neck

(Shiko, in Addiss et al. 1992: 66)

ikinagara / tonbo kawaku / ishi no ue

still alive / a dragonfly drying up / on a rock

(Uda, in Ueda 2003: 187)

kago no tori / cho wo urayamu / metsuki kana

the caged bird / envies the butterfly— / just look at its eyes

(Issa, in Addiss et al. 1992: 56)

shiragiku ni / tsutanaki chōzu / kakaru nari

white chrysanthemums! / they've pitched water on you / from the washing bowl

(Issa, in Mackenzie 1957: 57)

This compassion for all kinds of animals including birds, insects, and even plants, is the same compassion behind the word *itadakimasu*, spoken before meals thanking the plants and animals for giving up their lives. It is also behind the strong desire to avoid waste—not on the grounds of "sustainability" or any other abstraction, but because it means destruction of life, and all life is identical and valuable. With very few exceptions, haiku express positive regard to all forms of life. Issa even shows regard to fleas and mosquitoes:

nomi domo ni / Matsushima misete / nigasu zo yo

come on fleas / I'll show you Matsushima— / then let you go

(Mackenzie 1957: 84)

kabashiraya / kore mo nakereba / kosabishiki

swarms of mosquitoes— / but without them / it's a little lonely

(Issa, in Addiss et al. 1992: 82)

Positive regard is implied even when not expressed explicitly, for example:

araigami / onaji hinata ni / hachi shishite

washed hair— / in the same sunlight / a bee is dead

(Hashimoto, in Ueda 2003: 105)

Some might say this could mean, "Good, saved from being stung by killing the bee with the bathwater". There is no such ambiguity, however, because positive regard is so deeply built into the discourse of haiku that this can be nothing other than a tragedy.

Another feature of haiku is congruence, or genuineness: the ideal haiku is of a genuine encounter with nature, where the poet has experienced a sense of wonder, respect, empathy, compassion, connection, or a perception of "suchness," and reflects this experience as honestly and directly as possible. As Bashō explains, "However well phrased your poetry may be, if your feeling is not natural — if the object and yourself are separate — then your poetry is not true poetry but merely your subjective counterfeit" (Bashō, in Yuasa 1967: 33).

These three aspects — empathy, unconditional positive regard, and congruence, are the three "core" conditions of Rogers's (1961) person-centered counselling. This may not be coincidental, since Rogers was influenced by Zen (Brazier 1997). The discourse of haiku, then, suggests a relationship to nature similar to that between a person-centered counsellor and their client: allowing nature to flourish through its own power, in its own way, with appreciation and respect but minimal interference.

SIMPLICITY

The discourse of haiku does not simply treat nature as an aesthetic diversion, but places appreciation for nature as an alternative to overconsumption. Material simplicity is not considered a sacrifice, but instead appreciated as a realization of the cultural ideal of *wabi*. One single haiku captures the essence of *wabi*:

yado no haru / nani mo naki koso / nani mo are

in my hut this spring / there is nothing / there is everything

(Sodo, in Bowers 1996: 12)

The haiku poets did not only *speak* of the joy of simple living in their poems; it was genuinely how they lived. Stryk (1985: 15) describes how Bashō "gave up virtually all possessions, his only concern spiritual and artistic discovery." Of Issa, Mackenzie (1957: 23) writes that he "never ceased to proclaim himself a countryman, and by his frugal example to exclaim against the luxury and artificiality of the town."

If poetry in Japan sometimes strays into aesthetic considerations separate from everyday life, then Issa brings it firmly back, with the following haiku:

ora ga yo ya / sokora no kusa mo / mochi ni naru

this world of ours! / even the grasses over there / give us our *mochi* [sticky rice]

(in Mackenzie 1957: 49, translation adapted)

This poem was accompanied by the prose "It is for courtiers and the like to mourn the waning of the moon and to sing the praises of blossoms" (Issa, in Mackenzie 1957: 49).

———————————

Overall, the importance of the discourse of haiku is that, like a Zen *koan*, it uses language to encourage the reader to go beyond language, beyond the world of intellectual abstractions, and reconnect directly with the more-than-human world. The way it does this is to describe actual encounters with everyday nature, in straight present tense, using a minimal amount of metaphor and abstraction, placing poetic emphasis on individual animals and plants, representing them as agents of their own lives living according to their natures, with implicit assumptions of empathy and positive regard built into the discourse. This is in marked contrast to the discourse of environmentalism, where terms like "biotic resources" or "biomass appropriation" do not refer to anything as specific and imaginable in the world as a "frog" or a "bee."

Bate (2000: 283) believes that nature poetry can save the world: "If mortals dwell in that they save the earth and if poetry is the original admission of dwelling, then poetry is the place where we save the earth." But Rigby (2001: 19) counters this by saying, "What are poets for? I too would like to believe that poets can in some measure help us to 'save the Earth.' However, they will only be able to do so if we are prepared to look up and listen when they urge us to lift our eyes from the page."

The discourse of haiku shows a way to encourage readers to lift their eyes from the page, because the animals and plants that inhabit the haiku also inhabit the local environment of the readers, and the readers are bound to come across them in their everyday lives. When they do, they may, if the haiku is successful, treat those inhabitants with the careful observation, empathy, and respect that the poet showed.

Ecologically, the discourse encourages learning from the ways of nature rather than violating them, which, according to Capra (1997), is the necessary foundation of a sustainable society. Most importantly, the approach to nature is a substitute for, not an addition to, a life spent obsessed by the pseudo-satisfiers of material possessions.

Haiku provides just one example of a discourse based on foundations that are very different from the abstractions employed by dominant discourses in the West. If language is necessarily a pale and distorted reflection of the reality it attempts to describe, then haiku is an attempt to minimize that distortion and point beyond itself, and beyond language, to more genuine relationships between humans, other animals, and nature.

This chapter has attempted not only to demonstrate *that* the discourse of haiku can help people reconnect with the reality of animals and the natural world, but also *how*. In other words, it described the cluster of discursive features that give the discourse the power to model and promote direct engagement with nature. The importance of showing how the discourse "works" is that it then becomes possible to take the cluster of features and apply some of them creatively in other discourses, even discourses that use other media.

In order to demonstrate this, the author created a collection of photographs that follow a visual grammar that is inspired by haiku. Photographs from the collection have been reproduced in black and white at the start of each chapter of the book, and color versions can be viewed at www.ecoling.net/photography1 .html. The collection is called *Chance Encounters*, an example of what could be called *Haiku-inspired photography* (see Stibbe 2005a).

All of the discourses described in the book so far have a visual dimension: animal product industries use technical pictures of machinery in their internal discourse and pictures of happy animals in fields in their external discourse; ecological science uses analytic diagrams where ecosystems are divided up into functional parts; animal rights discourse uses high-angle shots to look down on passive animals suffering in cages; environmental photography shows environmental destruction from a "god's-eye" objective view taken by helicopter; and conservation charities use close-up photographs of the faces of cuddly animals looking directly at the viewer to establish sympathetic relationships. The photographs in the *Chance Encounters* collection aim to provide an alternative visual discourse by drawing on the cluster of discursive features that make up linguistic haiku.

Like haiku poems, the photographs depict a moment of connection with ordinary nature, imbuing it with significance simply by framing it and saying "this is worthy of a poem/photograph." In haiku poetry, individual animals are given salience by being placed at the start (the theme) or the end (end focus) or having a whole line devoted just to their name. In haiku-inspired photography, animals are given salience by being presented in the foreground, in the center, and/or in colors that contrast with the background.

In the same way that haiku eschew metaphor, the photographs exhibit high photorealism and proportionately sized features, suggesting a literal rather than symbolic interpretation (Kress and van Leeuwen 1996: 110). The camera angle in the photographs is whatever is most natural when viewing the animals closely and attentively, that is, a neutral angle in most cases, but sometimes a slightly higher angle for very small animals or a lower angle for birds. Neutral angles reflect relationships of equality and emphasize the agency of the animals (Kress and van Leeuwen 1996: 146). In terms of perspective, the vanishing point is within the picture, which suggests engagement (Kress and van Leeuwen 1996: 142).

The shot is full, placing animals in what would be called "public space" if they were human, showing closeness but noninterference (Kress and van Leeuwen 1996: 130). The fullness of the shot places animals in the context of their surroundings, and elements within the photograph indicate the season it was taken in. In this way, the visual features of the photographs show the world as it would look to a viewer crouching down or peering up, looking carefully at commonplace animals without interfering with them, and in doing so finding something of value. Ultimately, the success of haiku-inspired photography depends on whether viewers start to look at the animals and plants they come across in their everyday life in new ways. The influence of the photography will therefore be strongest when it reflects the bioregion where the viewers live and directs their attention toward the beauty and value of the ordinary nature around them, which lies not in the photographs but in the animals and plants themselves.

Clusters of discursive principles drawn from haiku could be applied across a wide range of discourses, from poetry and literature to biology textbooks, with the aim of working against the erasure of animals and encouraging reconnection with nature. The next chapter describes how a particular discourse of Japanese animation embeds some of the principles of haiku within it, and can potentially be used for a radically different type of environmental education.

9

ZEN AND THE ART
OF ENVIRONMENTAL EDUCATION

The previous chapter described the discourse of haiku as an example of a discourse that represents the natural world in ways that overcome some of the abstraction and objectification of mainstream discourses in the West and promotes direct connection with animals and nature. However, haiku poetry itself is likely only to appeal to a small audience, given both difficulties in translation and the marginal place of poetry within popular culture. Photography is one way of using some of the characteristics of haiku to reach people, but there is another, even more powerful way, through moving images. This chapter explores a film discourse that has similarities with haiku. The focus is on one particular film — *Tonari no Totoro* (My Neighbour Totoro), and its potential for encouraging close relationships with nature.

Tonari no Totoro is a hand-drawn animated film produced by Miyazaki Hayao (NB: Japanese names are in the Japanese order of surname followed by first name) and released in Japan by Studio Ghibli in 1988 (Ghibli 1988). The film portrays the interaction of humans, nature, and forest spirits in rural Japan, and has gained a significant following due to what film critic Kanō Seiji describes as "its extremely original and powerfully persuasive ways of representing nature" (Kanō 1998 [NB: unless otherwise specified, all Japanese material has been translated by the author]). Some of Miyazaki's other films contain explicitly environmental themes such as habitat destruction, in *Heisei tanuki gassen ponpoko* (*The Racoon War*); pollution, in *Kaze no tani no Nausicaa* (*Nausicaa of the Valley of the Wind*); and deforestation, in *Mononoke-hime* (*Princess Mononoke*). *Tonari no Totoro*, however, has special importance, since the film models positive relationships between humans and nature rather than representing a breakdown of those relationships.

This chapter investigates whether, like *haiku*, *sadō* (the tea ceremony), *shodō* (calligraphy), and other cultural art forms, animation of the type used in *Tonari no Totoro* has the potential to draw out ecological insights from Zen and Shinto traditions and make them available to a popular audience. If so, it is an art form that has the power to cross borders. Indeed, *Tonari no Totoro* has been released in two English dubbed versions, one by Fox in 1993 (Fox 1993), and another, more recently, by Disney in 2006 (Disney 2006). The arrival of *Tonari no Totoro* with its Zen-like and subtly animistic portrayal of human interaction with nature, in the midst of a Western culture suffering increasing alienation from the natural world, brings with it the potential to contribute to new forms of environmental education.

As the ecological crisis worsens, the importance of environmental education across all educational contexts, formal and informal, for people of all ages, has become increasingly recognized. At the same time, some of the limitations of environmental education as it is usually envisaged have also come to light (Bowers 2001, Cooper 1992, Orr 1992, Smith and Williams 1999, Sterling 2001, Stone and Barlow 2005). One limitation is the way that environmental education tends toward statistics, technical knowledge, and global abstractions, without simultaneously grounding the abstract in concrete awareness of natural systems and the very real consequences of environmental destruction. The common injunction to "think globally, act locally" may be partly to blame, because a global "environment" is difficult to apprehend directly. David Yencken suggests a focus on both the global and the local:

> If we do not think locally, we may ignore rich sources of environmental knowledge and devalue local understanding and experience. . . . If we do not act globally, we will never solve the big issues of the global commons: atmospheric and ocean pollution (Yencken 2000: 4)

One benefit of thinking locally, and carefully observing the ecosystems of the local bioregion across the seasons, is a deeper understanding of the way that natural systems work. Perhaps even more importantly, close observation of animals and nature has the potential to help develop a firsthand understanding of the *value* of healthy natural systems, that is, the value of the flourishing of life. Without appreciation of value, knowledge and technical skills are directionless.

Fritjof Capra, a leading holistic scientist, recommends an approach to environmental education that includes both technical knowledge of ecological principles and the values that are necessary to guide that technical knowledge (Capra 2005: xiv). David Orr's concept of *ecoliteracy* is similar. In addition to the capacity to understand scientific principles, Orr suggests that ecoliteracy requires:

> the more demanding capacity to observe nature with insight. . . . People who do not know the ground on which they stand miss . . . the capacity to distinguish between health and disease in natural systems and their relationship to health and disease in human ones. If literacy is driven by the search for knowledge, ecological literacy is driven by the sense of wonder, the sheer delight in being alive in a beautiful, mysterious, bountiful world (Orr 1992: 354).

There is a danger that environmental education represents the environment only negatively, as something that can give us skin cancer because of holes in the ozone layer, or something that can poison us through pollution, or something that can flood our homes because of climate change. This is all vital, but it is also important to explore positive aspects of the environment, for example, the environment as a rich source of contact and connection with myriad other species. Connection with local natural systems offers the possibility not only of understanding and caring more about the ecosystems that support life, but also finding ways of fulfilling important human needs through appreciation of local nature rather than vainly trying to satisfy them through ever-increasing consumption.

Broadening a preoccupation with abstractions and toxins to include a more grounded form of direct understanding and appreciation of natural systems is not easy, however, because environmental education operates primarily through the medium of words. Overcoming the abstraction of words and encouraging direct unmediated experience is something that is at the core of Zen.

The term *Zen* is not limited to formal disciplines such as the *Rinzai* and *Sōtō* branches of Zen Buddhism, but encompasses ways of approaching life and aesthetics that have been influenced by Zen Buddhism and have become widely integrated into traditional Japanese culture. Matsuo Bashō is credited with infusing a Zen perspective into haiku poetry (Suzuki 1970: 239); Takeno Jō and his successor Sen Rikyū are described as weaving Zen into the tea ceremony (Sen 1979: 62); and Morihei Ueshiba, the founder of Aikido, is known for bringing Zen into martial arts. The meditative spirit of Zen, divorced from monastic rituals, has been incorporated into many other cultural forms, including poetry, the tea ceremony, architecture, pottery, calligraphy, painting, and landscape design. Animation may provide yet another path for Zen perspectives to become infused into everyday life, and contribute to environmental awareness.

Drawing on ecological perspectives across cultures and time spans is a treacherous path, however. There are those like Arthur Danto (1987) who claim that Eastern thinking is just too different from Western thinking ever to be assimilated, and those like Kalland (2002) and Saito (1992) who argue that Zen has failed to make Japan an ecologically responsible country and contains features that facilitate ecological degradation. Clearly, though, Zen was not designed specifically to address current ecological problems, and the question for environmental education is not whether Zen as a whole contributes to sustainability, but whether insights can be drawn from Zen to complement existing approaches and make them more effective at contributing to sustainability.

There are several aspects of Zen that could potentially be drawn on to contribute to environmental education. The ethicist Simon James sees in the Zen insistence on paying careful attention to phenomena something close to the environmentalist notion of intrinsic value (James 2003: 156, 2004: 83). Robert Carter similarly describes how the locus of Zen ethics extends beyond human relational concerns to appreciation of and responsibility for the natural world, claiming that the self expanded (or disbanded) through Zen practice "identifies

with the greater whole, seeks to preserve it, cherish it, is emotionally enrap-
tured by it and cares about its wellbeing" (Carter 2001: 115). Such identification
could, in turn, lead to the "Zen ideals of simplicity, frugality, and poverty in
relation to land use so that nature is not exploited out of selfish motivations"
(Odin 1997: 100).

It is, of course, arguable whether Zen contains "ethics" or "ideals" as such,
but for environmental education, what may have most potential is Zen's insistence on direct experience of what D. T. Suzuki (1970) calls "isness" or "suchness," and James (2003: 156) calls "the thing at hand—the thing in its thus-
ness." If these expressions seem clumsy, it is because they are trying to hint
toward something that can never be expressed in words—a direct appreciation
of reality unmediated by language and concepts. Environmental education is
usually highly mediated, exposing students primarily to words rather than to
actual plants, animals, and natural systems. The words themselves often lack
referents that can be sensually experienced or imagined: the term "environment" itself is one of them, as are terms like "biomass appropriation," "habitat loss," "endangered species," "ecosystem" and "biodiversity" (Bourke and
Meppem 2000: 299). On the other hand, Zen may offer the possibility of a more
direct, sensual and phenomenological experience of natural systems, as an essential complement to more abstract ways of knowing. Suzuki explains that:

> Zen does not . . . indulge in abstraction or in conceptualisation. . . .
> When the mind, now abiding in its isness . . . free from intellectual com-
> plexities . . . surveys the world of the senses in all its multiplicities, it
> discovers in it all sorts of values hitherto hidden from sight. Here opens
> to the artist a world full of wonders. (1970: 16–17)

The question is whether Japanese animation, like other forms of Japanese
art, has the potential to encourage direct experience of natural systems and
open people up to the sense of wonder identified by authors such as Suzuki and
Orr as well as Rachel Carson (1998/1956). If so, the further question arises of
whether animation can contribute cross-culturally to environmental education

through translation into other languages. These questions are explored through analysis of *Tonari no Totoro* in both its original Japanese version and two English translations.

Miyazaki Hayao, the producer of *Tonari no Totoro*, is well known for interweaving deep ecological themes and aspects of traditional Japanese culture into his films. Although he has not formally trained in Zen or Shinto, he clearly has a deep respect for both. The following passage reveals his familiarity with and fondness of Shinto animism:

> In my grandparents' time, it was believed that spirits [*kami*] existed everywhere — in trees, rivers, insects, wells, anything. My generation does not believe this, but I like the idea that we . . . should treasure everything because there is a kind of life to everything (Miyazaki, in Boyd and Nishimura 2004: 16).

While the environmental message of *Tonari no Totoro* is not as explicit as some of his other films, it is clear that Miyazaki did intend *Tonari no Totoro* to provide environmental insights. In a 1988 interview, shortly before the film was released, he expressed the motivation behind the film as follows:

> [*Tonari no Totoro* is] for children and their parents to watch together; it is about Japan; it is about the place that they live in, and it is a film which allows parents and children to communicate together. Of course, it had to be a fun and exciting movie, but at the same time, I wanted it to be a film where viewers relate Japan's future environmental and ecological problems to the condition of the society which surrounds them (Miyazaki 1988).

In other words, the film is designed to encourage the kind of intergenerational dialogue about the value of disappearing local ecosystems and cultural traditions that is essential for environmental education.

The plot of *Tonari no Totoro* is relatively straightforward. Two girls (Mei and Satsuki, age five and eleven) move to the countryside with their father to be nearer to their mother, who is hospitalized with an illness. In exploring their new world, they encounter, with delight, a wide range of natural and supernatu-ral phenomena, from tadpoles to the giant forest spirit *Totoro*. The *Totoro* and the *Catbus* (a creature who is an unusual cross between a cat and a bus) help the girls when Mei gets lost en route to visit her mother in the hospital.

Tonari no Totoro is entirely hand-drawn animation, a medium that allows intricate and detailed artwork for elements that are relatively static, but cruder drawing for elements that move (Lamarre 2002). This immediately separates elements into two groups: the intricate and the simplified. The human charac-ters and the supernatural creatures are all drawn in the simplified style: line drawings filled in with unmodulated and relatively saturated colours. On the other hand, all natural elements are drawn in the intricate style: the colors are highly modulated, involving many different shades with complex patches of shadow. Aside from small yellow, blue, or purple flowers, and the blue of the sky, the colors used in the intricate style are mostly subdued, natural shades of green and brown, resulting in extremely realistic portrayals of nature in rural Japan.

The majority of backgrounds in the film show common wild plants, trees, and summer flowers, mixed with areas of agricultural land and houses or shrines made from local materials such as wood and rush. These are all depicted in an in-tricate, realistic style, emphasizing how human cultivation and artifacts were an integral part of local ecosystems in traditional Japan. The humans are depicted in the simplified style, making them appear separate from their surroundings, which is a potential disadvantage for environmental education, since it fails to capture human embeddedness in natural systems. It does, however, highlight the realness and beauty of the natural world, without letting nature become overshadowed by the human characters or the appealing, fantastic creatures.

The separation between humans and nature created by the dual modality of the film is partially compensated for through visual techniques. One such technique involves medium or long shots of human characters, with wild plants at the bottom in the immediate foreground, the humans behind them in the mid-foreground, and trees and fields in the background. This technique helps to make the human characters appear more embedded in their environment. In ad-dition, the film does not portray phenomena as existing separately, but instead represents a complex interaction between humans, nonhuman nature, sacred elements, and supernatural creatures. The discussion below describes these four central aspects of the film and their relationship with each other.

THE NATURAL

Nearly all scenes in the film include intricately drawn, realistic aspects of nature: groves of wild trees, rice fields, wild plants, flowers, animals, clouds, rain, rocks, and streams. In some cases these are in the background, adding beauty while the focus is on the activities and goals of the characters. This represents a superficial relationship with nature, where nature provides nice scenery while the mind is preoccupied with other things. Some scenes focus on natural phenomena only, but use them to give a semiotic message: a gradually lightening sky indicates a new day has started; a shot of dark clouds indicates that rain is about to fall; birds fly across the sunset, indicating that darkness will soon overcome the lost Mei.

Importantly, though, the film also incorporates a different way of representing nature where, for one continuous shot, the focus is intently on natural phenomena, depicted for their own sake rather than for the sake of adding a fact to the story. In one such moment, there is a cut from the truck carrying the family to their new house, to a shot of a stream. A single green leaf floats down the stream into a small waterfall; the water glints in the sunshine and the only sound is that of the water. The contrast is clear: the movement of the family is purposeful, with the goal of arriving at the new house, which is an essential step in the plot of the film. The leaf, on the other hand, floats along the stream without obvious purpose, its significance being purely in itself.

A leaf floating in a stream is exactly the kind of small natural occurrence that the audience may miss in their everyday lives as they rush around serving their own purposes. When watching the film, however, they are forced to notice the leaf, and their attention is drawn to it though its central position, by its color salience (a green leaf in a brown river), by its movement, and because it is framed by the banks and rocks. It is also framed in time, since there is a definite cut to the leaf from a quite different scene (the truck), and a definite cut away after the leaf falls (a return to the truck).

The framing of a minute part of ordinary nature, depicted artistically yet realistically, is a way of imbuing it with significance and value, encouraging a form of environmental consciousness that appreciates local nature down to the smallest detail. There are many such scenes in the film: a butterfly flits in from the top right hand corner and settles on a flower in the center; a snail slithers up the stem of a pumpkin leaf; a drop of water falls into a stream, ripples spreading out in all directions; a frog walks slowly from left to right across the center of the screen in the rain; a drop of rain falls in a puddle with an audible plop; a frog slowly lets out a deep croak.

In all of these scenes the natural phenomenon being framed for special attention is moving, but is painstakingly drawn in the intricate and realistic mode of drawing, making these scenes particularly realistic in contrast with the simplified style of human characters. Evidence that Miyazaki places importance on these natural shots can be found in the original theatrical trailer to the film, which is a montage of the most visually appealing parts of the film, and includes several of these shots.

There are strong parallels between the framing of nature in these moments in the film and in the Zen-based tradition of haiku. First, both haiku and the nature shots are brief, lasting around four seconds, and focus on just one particular animal, plant, or other aspect of nature. Second, in both cases the focus is on framing ordinary nature, of the kind people come across in their everyday life. Third, and most important, the framing is done in an artistic way that reveals the hidden beauty of the ordinary. Frogs, butterflies, leaves, streams, snails, and the sounds of water are common themes in haiku. The following haiku, by Bashō, is one of the most famous:

furuike ya / kawazu tobikomu / mizu no oto
an old pond / a frog leaps in / sound of the water

In a major movement within haiku writing, championed most prominently by the last of the four "grand masters" of haiku poetry, Shiki, toward the end of the nineteenth century, metaphor and symbol are carefully avoided, and phenomena of nature are depicted as genuinely as possible. Odin puts this eloquently in his description of the poetry of the twelfth-century *waka* poet, Saigyō:

> The aesthetic and spiritual symbols of Saigyō's nature poetry do not point beyond themselves to a transcendent or supra-sensible reality over and above the natural world, but fully contain the reality which they symbolize (1997: 103).

And so too for a large number of nature haiku, in which animals and plants are represented doing what they naturally do, with no ulterior or superimposed meaning. In *Tonari no Totoro*, the frog appears as a frog and not a symbol of something else, croaking as frogs do rather than talking or acting unusually; the snail slithers; the butterfly flits; the leaf floats down the stream. This is nature *sonomama* (as it is), which Suzuki (1970: 230) explains is consonant with the Buddhist ideal of *tathata* (suchness).

THE HUMAN

Whether or not nature haiku include explicit reference to people, there is always an implied human presence. This is because haiku record the poet's genuine encounters with nature. Unrecorded in Bashō's haiku about the frog (above), though undoubtedly present, is Bashō's ear hearing the sound of the water. Likewise, in the visual haiku of *Tonari no Totoro*, the viewing angle is always from the perspective a human viewer might take: a viewer standing on the bank looking at the leaf in the stream or closely observing the movement of the snail, following the flitting of the butterfly with their eyes or crouching down to see the frog. In this way, the film records not just nature, but the act of "seeing" nature, and places the viewer in the role of the seer.

In several places in the film, the observers of nature are explicitly depicted as Mei and Satsuki. This is achieved by picturing the children with postures and facial expressions showing that they are intensely looking at something, and then cutting to a shot of what they are looking at. An instance of this occurs in

one scene that begins with the two girls leaning over the rail of a bridge looking intently at the stream below, their eyes forming invisible vectors pointing
downward. There is then a cut to a shot of some small, ordinary fish sparkling
in the water below, from a high angle — the angle that the girls are looking
from — which places the viewer in the position of seeing the scene through the
eyes of the girls. The next cut is back to the girls, showing the reaction on their
faces. The reaction is one of pleasure and delight, and so the film is showing the
viewer how to look at and find delight in nature.

There are many shots in the film where delighted reactions to nature are
modelled: Mei and Satsuki stare wide-eyed at an acorn that glints in the sunshine, and Satsuki says the word *donguri* (acorn); Mei looks intently at tadpoles
in a pond saying the word *ojamatakushi* (a mispronunciation of *otamajakushi*, tadpole). In another scene both children stare with delight at an enormous camphor
tree as it is shown from a low angle, with the view slowly panning up to the top.
This depiction demonstrates to viewers in a very physical way how to look at a
tree — starting with its trunk and moving upward to the leaves and branches,
and experiencing pleasure.

The girls' way of approaching the world has strong parallels with the form
of ecological consciousness that Ishizawa and Fernández (2002: 21) call "Loving
the world as it is," which they contrast with Western abstraction. The key is a
particular way of looking closely at nature, without which people will always
be observing at a distance. As Suzuki explains:

> Most people do not really know how to look at the flower; for one thing
> they stand away from it. . . . The one who beholds is separated from
> the object which is beheld; there is an impassable gap between the two
> and it is impossible for the beholder to come in touch inwardly with his
> object (1970: 353).

The girls' way of seeing becomes particularly salient through its contrast
with the very different way that their father interacts with the world. The
father, a university professor, clearly *knows about* the world, while the two girls
actually *see* it. The girls are therefore interacting in a more Zen-like way with

the world than their father; as Hagen says, "the buddha-dharma [teaching] is about *seeing*, not about believing" (Hagen 1999: 49).

At one point in the film, Satsuki in the foreground stares in wonder at the camphor tree and exclaims, *"Otōsan, sugoi ki"* ("Father, amazing tree!"). The father is busy and gives the tree only the most miniscule of glances before turning away and saying, *"Kusu no ki da yo"* ("It's a camphor tree, you know"), using the authoritative particle *yo*. He looks at an acorn that the girls find, not with their sense of wonder, but with intellectual curiosity, saying, *"Risu iru kanā"* ("I wonder if there's a squirrel here."). When Mei and Satsuki encounter soot sprites, he is quick to explain they are *makkurokurosuke*, occurring when eyes adjust to a dark place, and later he explains that the Totoro is the *mori no nushi* (keeper of the forest), yet he can see neither the soot sprites nor the Totoro.

The study where the father works, oblivious to the wonders of a tree magically growing outside his window, is full of books and papers, but there are no natural objects whatsoever. In one scene, Mei comes into his study from playing outside contentedly and places six flowers on his desk, as if prompting him to notice the natural world outside of his books. And he does, by picking up and appreciating the flower. The father, then, is deeply knowledgeable, but without Mei's help does not "see," and so misses out on the sense of wonder that the two girls experience.

The girls' direct, intuitive approach to experiencing the world comes across clearly when a comparison is made between the way that the girls speak in the original Japanese version of the film compared to the English translations in the two dubbed versions. When Mei and Satsuki stand on the bridge and look intently at the fish, Satsuki says, *"Sakana! hora, mata hikatta"* ("Fish! look, they glimmered again") in the original Japanese version. However, the Zen feeling of unity in the relationship between girls and fish is lost in the English translation of the Fox version when Mei is made to say "What are those little things swimming around?" and Satsuki is made to answer "I don't know. Goldfish maybe or something." This exchange exemplifies a questioning, knowledge-based approach, rather than an intuitive approach based on a sense of wonder. There are several similar instances of this in table 9.1.

TABLE 9.1 **English Dubbing Compared to Japanese Original**

ORIGINAL JAPANESE	ENGLISH DUBBING
Sakana! hora, mata hikatta	What are those little things swimming around?
(Fish! look, they glimmered again)	(Fox)
Otōsan, sugoi ki! (Father, an amazing tree!)	Dad, what's that big tree? (Disney)
Minna ni wa mienai n da wa (No one can see it)	But how come nobody can see the bus? (Fox)
Obake yashiki mitai (It's like a ghost house)	Do you think it's haunted? (Fox)
Ki ga yoketeru (The trees are parting)	But how does he make it do that? (Fox)
Ki ga nai (There's no tree)	What happened to the tree? (Fox)

In all these cases, the children in the Japanese version are verbalizing their direct sensual experience — expressing the world *sonomama*, as it is. In the English version, however, they are abstracting away from their experience to discover underlying patterns or causes, which is closer to a Western scientific approach. As Suzuki points out:

> Concepts are useful in defining the truth of things, but not in making us personally acquainted with it. . . . The idea that the ultimate truth of life and of things generally is to be intuitively and not conceptually grasped . . . is what the Zen form of Buddhism has contributed (Suzuki 1970: 219).

The intuitive and appreciative approach to the world that the girls exemplify could be considered a manifestation of the Zen aesthetics of *wabi* and *sabi*. Together, these aesthetics could be described as "an intuitive appreciation of a transient beauty in the physical world. . . . It is an understated beauty that exists in the modest, rustic, imperfect, or even decayed (Juniper 2003: 51). In other words, worth is recognized in things that are not valuable in a material or utilitarian sense: a leaf, a tadpole, a dilapidated old shrine, a rough earthen bowl. Ecologically, *wabi* and *sabi* are important because human needs are satisfied without the endless, and ultimately self-defeating, accumulation of shiny new possessions.

Wabi is demonstrated in the film through reaction shots showing the children's delight in ordinary nature, and in the run-down human artifacts around them. When they first see their new house they say, *"Ano uchi?"* ("That house?") and shout *"boro!"* ("run-down!"), but with extreme pleasure in their voices and facial expressions. They find the wooden porch is rotten and again react with delight as they say, *"Kussatteru!"* ("It's rotten!"). Similarly, when Mei finds an old bucket she beams with happiness, saying, *"Soko nuke da!"* ("It doesn't have a bottom!"), before using it as a telescope. The Disney version entirely misses the sense of *wabi*, however, by translating *Soko nuke da* (It doesn't have a bottom) as "What a stupid bucket!"

In another scene, the Fox version loses the sense of *wabi* by representing pleasure in possession rather than in appreciating things as they are. When Satsuki and Mei stare intently at an acorn, Satsuki simply says, *"Donguri"* ("Acorn") in the Japanese version. However, the Fox version dubs this as "Hey Mei, look, an acorn" and then makes Mei respond with "But I want an acorn too," despite Mei's silence in the original. Later Mei says the single word *"Atta"* ("There's one"), which becomes translated as "Oh, I have my own acorn right here." In this way the acorns become human property, rather than simply existing as objects of wonder in themselves.

The use of the pronoun "I" and the possessive "my" in "I have my own acorn" suggests an egotistical concentration on self rather than on what is being observed. This is also apparent in the Fox translation of Satsuki's comment *"Heya no naka de donguri ga ochiteru no"* ("Acorns are falling in the room"), which becomes "Acorns! We found them! And I found a bunch of them right near the back door." In this case, the original Japanese makes the acorns the agent of the clause, but the English translation makes the girls refer to themselves as agents. Similarly, when the father suggests that the acorns may have been left by a mouse, Mei says, *"Risu ga ii"* ("A squirrel is better") in the original Japanese, with squirrel as the subject of the clause. The Fox version, however, makes the clause center around Mei and her desires: "Yuk. But I don't want a dumb rat."

Indeed, the pronoun "I" is used 178 times in the Fox dub, but rarely are equivalent pronouns used in the original Japanese. This is partly because Japanese sentences do not require subjects to be made explicit, but also because the characters in the English version interpret the world through themselves and their desires rather than directly. If Zen "abhors egoism in any form of assertion," as Suzuki claims (1970: 225), then the girls in the English version fail to achieve this Zen state of egoless absorption in the world. The girls in the Japanese version, however, come far closer to this state, exhibiting the form of ecological consciousness that deep ecologist Arne Naess once described as: "to enmesh yourself in what you are doing, what you experience, in such a way that the relation to your ego disappears, and the Self is expanded into the World" (Naess, in Loy 1998: 105).

Another form of ecological practice exhibited in the film is the way the children demonstrate the Buddhist conception of *naikan* in relationship to food. *Naikan* is reflection and resulting gratitude and appreciation for all that is sacrificed so that we can live (Jones and O'Neil 2002). In the case of food, *naikan* can lead to ecologically beneficial behaviors such as the consumption of locally produced organic food, with wastage carefully avoided.

The children exhibit *naikan* when they discover the field where the Grandma character grows vegetables, showing their appreciation by saying "*Obāchan no hatake tte takara no yama mitai*" ("Grandma's field is like a mountain of treasure"). Before eating tomatoes and cucumber cooled in the stream, the girls say, "*itadakimasu,*" the traditional Japanese phrase that indicates appreciation for the plants that have given up their lives and the people who went to the effort of growing them. The food is fresh and simple and the reaction on the girls' faces is portrayed as great enjoyment. This is a particularly important scene, because other aspects of the appreciation of nature that manifest themselves in the film could be accused of being aesthetic and noninterventionist, thus glossing over the very real need of humans to interfere with nature to create food, and the ethical questions this raises.

Predictably, the Disney version loses the concept of *naikan*, by translating "*Obāchan no hatake tte takara no yama mitai*" ("Grandma's field is like a mountain of treasure") as "Wow, Granny, your garden is just like a market." Even more distant from the concept of *naikan*, the Disney dub translates *itadakimasu* as "On your marks, get set, go!" as if eating was a race rather than a deep appreciation of sacrifice.

Overall, the words of the human characters in the Japanese version combine with the rich depictions of the natural world to demonstrate deep connection with nature. The frequent failure of the English dubbing to capture this connection is a loss in terms of the English version's ability to contribute to environmental education, but also something of a gain in its potential for highlighting key differences in culture with regard to nature.

THE SACRED

Shinto animism is subtly interwoven throughout the film, most significantly through the depiction of Shinto symbols surrounding one particular tree that plays an important role in the film. This enormous *kusu no ki* (camphor tree) stands next to a dilapidated Shinto shrine, and the sacredness of the tree is marked by a rice-rope and paper streamers wrapped around its trunk. The tree's sacredness is further emphasized in a scene where the girls and their father bow to it, thanking it for looking after Mei, while the father speaks of a time when humans and trees were *naka yoshi* (on good terms).

There are other Shinto symbols throughout the film: the truck in the first scene drives past a roadside shrine; there are paper streamers next to the Totoro inside the camphor tree; shrine gates (*torii*) are shown at the foot of a hill; there is a roadside *ojizo san* statue that the girls bow to when waiting for their father's return; Mei sits under a line of *ojizo-san* when she is lost; a fox spirit shrine (*inari jinja*) gives Mei a chill as she looks at it. No words are spoken about the Shinto elements in the film — they are just there, blended in with nature and experienced as the children experience them. This leads analyst Helen McCarthy (1999: 122) to conclude that "*My Neighbor Totoro*'s plot deliberately sidelines religion in favor of nature." Susan Napier disagrees, however, feeling that "Shinto's animistic spirit clearly infiltrates the film" (Napier 2001: 491).

Rather than "infiltrating" the film, Shinto could be considered integral to the film because it is part of the spiritual geography of traditional Japan, blending in with nature in ways which make it impossible to say where religion stops and nature starts (on such boundaries, see Taylor 2007). Shinto symbols are made from natural materials and gain their meaning from their particular location in a natural setting—a rock, a waterfall, a tree, the top of a mountain. The symbols may be representations of *kami* (gods/spirits), but, again, there is no dividing line between *kami* and nature. As the eighteenth-century Shinto thinker Motōri Norinaga said, "*Kami* can be the Sun Goddess, the spirit of a great man, a tree, a cat, a fallen leaf" (in Kerr 2002: 32).

Miyazaki stated that he did not conceive of *kami* as some kind of literal spirit but felt a "very warm appreciation for the various, very humble rural Shinto rituals that continue to this day throughout rural Japan" (Miyazaki, in Boyd and Nishimura 2004: 8). In *Tonari no Totoro* it is significant that only the children interact with *kami* in their explicit form (the *Totoros*) and in their implicit form (as elements of nature such as trees and fish). This is related to the purity of their *kokoro*, a term that encompasses both mind and heart, without a Cartesian split between them. As Boyd and Nishimura (2004: 9) explain:

> Shinto understands the whole of life, including both humans and nature, as creative and life giving. . . . Manifestations of this generative, vital power [are] called *kami*. . . . However, to experience the *kami* presence of any one of these aspects of nature requires an aesthetically pure and cheerful heart/mind (*kokoro*), an emotional, mental and volitional condition that is not easily attained (Boyd and Nishimura 2004: 9).

Without any words in the film about Shinto practices, what is left is the sense of sacredness of place: it is clear that those who wrapped a paper streamer around a tree or placed a shrine at the top of a mountain had some kind of respect for the place and the life that exists within the place.

THE FANTASTIC

Tonari no Totoro goes beyond the established religious symbols that mark sacredness of place to invent new, moving, fantastic creatures: the giant Totoro, smaller Totoros, the Catbus, and the Soot Sprites. There is a complex relationship between the film's supernatural beings and its sacred elements. The placing of Totoro within a tree surrounded by a Shinto streamer suggests that the Totoro is a form of nature-spirit or *kami*, as does the way that the father refers to him as *mori no nushi* (keeper of the forest). However, in terms of physical form and persona, the Totoro is far removed from anything in Japanese Shinto tradition, and is separated from the Shinto aspects in the film by being drawn in the simplified style. An important consideration is whether the supernatural creatures contribute to the ecological insights of the film, or whether they are attention-grabbing elements that distract viewers away from relationships with the natural world.

Film critics use various terms to describe the fantastic/supernatural creatures who appear in *Tonari no Totoro*. Hirashima (1997) calls them *seirei*, literally spirit-ghosts, with the character *rei* associating them with spirits of the dead. Kiridōshi (2001: 39) uses the term *mononoke*, making them seem to be somewhat vengeful spirits. The term that seems most appropriate, though, is the one used by Kanō (1998), *yōsei*, meaning Faerie (*yō* meaning magical and *sei* meaning spirit in the sense of heart/mind/spirit). The way that Ted Andrews describes Faeries shows a clear parallel to the fantastic elements of *Tonari no Totoro*:

> The world still holds an ancient enchantment. It hints of journeys into unseen and unmapped domains. . . . There was a time when . . . each cavern and hollow tree was a doorway to another world. Humans recognized life in all things . . . every blade of grass and flower had a tale to tell. Now we no longer see with a child's or seer's eyes (Andrews 1993: 3).

Indeed, the *Totoro*'s name comes from Mei's mispronunciation of the *troll* of Norse legend. Trolls are Faeries in the original sense of wild and powerful spirits symbolizing the forces of nature, from a time before the fairy became fictionalized and trivialized. It could be argued that modern fairies are made-up characters that lead children into a brief spell of enchantment before they are pulled out into the rational adult world, literally disenchanted, by being told that fairies do not exist (Stibbe 2005b).

Tonari no Totoro could be equally accused of creating fictional fairies that lead to only a temporary sense of enchantment. However, as Kiridōshi (2001: 39) points out, the children in the film are enchanted not only by the supernatural creatures, but also by the ordinary elements in nature around them. These natural elements are represented in realistic, intricate drawings, compared to the simplified line-drawing style of the Totoros that highlights their fictional nature. Enchantment with ordinary nature, rather than fairies, is the "indestructible" sense of wonder that Rachel Carson (1998/1956: 40) believed is the most precious gift that can be given to children. The Faeries in the film give a sense of enchantment, of wonder, but the ultimate message is that the enchantment is there too in ordinary nature, if one only looks.

From a Zen perspective, it is significant that the fantastic creatures do not talk and therefore cannot convey abstractions or conceptualizations but only feelings such as wonder, which can carry across into the natural settings in which they are embedded. Shimizu (1997: 96) believes that "if Totoro conveyed meaning by speaking like a human, the relationship with Mei and Satsuki would suddenly become trivial (*tsumaranai*)." It is also significant that the main characters in the film are children. As the marine biologist and environmentalist, Rachel Carson, suggested:

> The child's world is fresh and new and beautiful, full of wonder and excitement. It is our misfortune that for most of us that clear-eyed vision, that true instinct for what is beautiful and awe-inspiring, is dimmed and even lost before we reach adulthood. (Carson 1998/1956: 40)

Of all the characters, it is only the children who can see Totoro and the other creatures. This provides a powerful metaphor: not only are the fantastic creatures invisible to the adults, the trees and flowers and ordinary nature are invisible too, simply because the adults are so concerned with other things that they do not look. Napier (2001: 128) points out that, "A young girl's fresh and clear-eyed perception of the world is the key to *Totoro*. The film is an invitation to adults to look; to see the world through the child's eyes and regain their lost sense of wonder.

———————————

This chapter began by noting that while mainstream environmental education may excel at imparting facts about global environmental problems, the scientific and technical language it is couched in often holds it back from encouraging close observation and appreciation of local ecosystems. There is something contradictory about using any medium, whether it is scientific language, poetry, or animation, to represent nature, if the aim is for students to learn from nature. The representation can never substitute for the intricate patterns of sights, smells, sounds, and touch that can be experienced directly. Even if students are brought into the middle of nature on a field trip, there is still a need for them to find ways of "seeing" into the core of that nature, rather than questioning and measuring and abstracting away from what is in front of their eyes. As Stephen Sterling points out, in the context of sustainable education, "we need to 'see' differently if we are to know and act differently, and . . . we need learning experiences to facilitate this change of perspective' (Sterling 2001: 52).

The analysis of the film *Tonari no Totoro* suggests that animation, in a way similar to haiku, can frame ordinary aspects of nature, using lines, colors, focus, and movement to highlight their significance and represent them from the angle of a human observer looking intently at them. Animation can therefore force the viewer into the position of crouching down to look at a frog, or looking slowly up a tree from roots to branches, guiding their eyes and modelling a way of seeing nature. Even more powerfully, animation can cut to humans looking at the scene, and portray their reaction, showing how people can receive delight and pleasure from interacting with the nature around them.

Tonari no Totoro uses these and a variety of other techniques to encourage a form of ecological consciousness closely attuned with local ecosystems, where human needs are met through participation in nature rather than material accumulation. Importantly, there is nothing "special" about the nature represented in the film: what appears is not the spectacular gorges of Shikoku; the colourful and intricate temples of Nikkō; the elegantly shaped Mount Fuji; the pine islands of Matsushima; or rare animals such as bears, eagles, or monkeys. Instead there are weeds along the edge of the road; common flowers such as irises and azaleas; and snails, frogs, and butterflies. The form of nature described in the film is available to most people within walking distance of their homes, even if only in a local park or a disused lot.

There are many aspects of environmental education not engaged in the film, of course. It does not mention the destruction of ecosystems and no prescriptions are offered. Yet the film does offer a model of relationships with the natural world that could help provide a basis for a better understanding of natural systems, a more caring approach to them, and a way of satisfying human needs without overconsumption.

In Japan, there are few people among the general population who are willing to participate in the meditation, austerity, and vegetarianism of formal Zen Buddhism. However, the insights of Zen reach deep into the culture through the tea ceremony, haiku, art, crafts, and traditional architecture. Certain forms of Japanese animation have the potential to provide an additional boundary-crossing medium through which Zen's encouragement of direct awareness of nature could revitalize aspects of traditional Japanese culture for a new generation of Japanese, as well as provide valuable perspectives for environmental education around the world. As Shinobu Price points out, "Those who love to watch anime, whether they know it or not, are participating in a widespread global exchange that may just have greater implications than they could ever have thought" (Price 2001: 168).

Conclusion

This book has examined destructive discourses that objectify animals and justify intensive farming systems, with negative consequences for both animals and the ecological systems that support life. It has explored counter-discourses of environmentalism and animal rights that attempt to deal with those consequences, but often fail to break free from the assumptions of destructive discourses. And it has considered discourses from lyrical science writing and traditional Japanese culture as examples of alternatives that could potentially inspire reconnection with animals and the natural world.

The significance of the book lies in the detailed linguistic analysis of the discourses, which reveals the cluster of discursive features that makes them "work." This means that the conclusion can go beyond a primitive suggestion that we simply dispose of destructive discourses and replace them wholesale with alternative discourses. It would be absurd, for example, to write an instruction manual for pork farming in lyrical prose or an environmental textbook in haiku. Instead, the conclusion is that it is possible to draw from the cluster of discursive features that make up alternative discourses and apply them creatively in writing, photographing, filming, or otherwise representing the world. The spirit of haiku, for example, could infuse a wide range of texts from biology textbooks to nature documentaries.

The book has focused primarily on written text, but that is certainly not to deny the importance of oral discourses. In fact, as Abram (1996) points out, oral discourses are often far more embedded in place than written discourses and provide a promising avenue in the search for alternative discourses. Another important dimension, which was only touched on in chapters 8 and 9, is visual communication (Franklin 2007; Baker 2001). If we are to overcome the erasure of animals we will have to transcend the symbolic and look at them directly. While photographs and films are always representations, they can model ways of looking at the world that viewers can apply to their own lives, and do so more directly than writing. A photograph of an animal places the viewer in the same physical orientation to the subject as the photographer was when the picture was taken, and this can convey something of the relationship between the photographer and subject.

Berger (1980) entitled his influential essay "Why look at animals?" but is accused by Burt (2005: 206) of not answering this question. The ecosophy that evolved throughout the course of this book could answer it in this way: "Why look at animals?"—because in doing so we realize our commonality with other animals. We realize that we too are embodied beings who depend for our continued existence on interrelationships with other organisms and the physical environment around us. "Why look at animals?"—because if we do not we might overlook the fact that we are violating their nature, something that inevitably leads to their suffering as well as ecological damage. "Why look at animals?"—because we can improve our mental health by contact with the nature around us, and find ways to fulfil higher human needs without excess consumption. "Why look at animals?"—because in their natural state animals fit seamlessly into ecosystems that absorb energy only from the sun and produce no waste, and we could gain inspiration for designing sustainable human systems in similar ways. And ultimately "Why look at animals?"—to discover who we are, because the alternative is to carve out a sense of self through searching for commonality and contrast with a set of signs and symbolic representations of animals rather than the animals themselves.

It was within this ecological philosophy—ecosophy—that discourses were analyzed. Detailed linguistic analysis was carried out to reveal the models of the world that discourses are based on, and these models were compared with the ecosophy. The key aspect was the power of discourse to erase animals and replace them with simulacra—copies without an original. In both destructive discourses and counter-discourses, individual animals were seen to be replaced by machines, objects, and resources and viewed only en mass as species or as part of the "environment" that surrounds humans. On the other hand, alternative discourses were shown to come closer to providing a "reflection of a profound reality" (Baudrillard 1994: 6). These reflections, although still representations, model direct relationships with animals.

There are many other possible ecosophies that discourses could be measured against, and each analyst will have their own. The central point is that an ecosophy, by definition, goes beyond the narrow focus on human-human relationships that much of social science is based on and includes consideration of the life-sustaining relationships among humans, animals, plants, and the physical environment. Even if the reader disagrees with the particular ecosophy that the analyses in this book are based on, and disagrees with the details of the analyses, it is hoped that the book still has value in the way that it has modelled ecological discourse analysis. Through ecological discourse analysis the models that underlie an inhumane and unsustainable society can be exposed, challenged, and resisted. Resistance of destructive discourses could take the form of personal resistance through, for example, a refusal to follow mainstream ways of conceptualizing animals as resources, machines, or passive objects — mentally rejecting these constructions when they are encountered in texts. It could involve more active resistance such as helping authors become aware of the ways that their texts are representing animals, and calling attention to unrecognized and undesirable side effects of those representations. Or resistance could involve searching for alternative discourses, discovering how they "work," and infusing their spirit into a wide range of new oral and written texts. This concluding chapter ends with an illustration of how some members of one particular professional group, conservationists, have become more critical about the language used by their profession and are seeking out new alternatives.

———————————

This book started with the conservationist Bergman mourning the erasure of animals as they become mere beeps on a radio-telemetry device. He criticizes not only the technology and its impact on relationships with animals, but also the discourse of surveillance that radio-telemetry facilitates:

> The language of our concern is at the same time the language of our dismissal of the animals, pushing them into the same category as the illegal aliens, enemies of state, and outlaws (Bergman 2005: 264).

Bergman is not the only conservationist who is disenchanted with the direction that the discourse of conservation is taking. The journal *ECOS: A Review of Conservation* contains a number of articles written by conservationists who are frustrated with the managerial, hypertechnical nature of the discourse that structures their profession. Their insights into language and connection with nature are illuminating. Oates (2008), for instance, writes that:

> Nature conservation can seriously damage your mental health, for working within today's wildlife and environmental movement can sever personal relationships with the world of Nature. . . . I suspect that we have paid so much attention to the (rapid) development of the scientific, ecological idiolect . . . that we have lost contact with our core language—the poetic language of passion for, of, with and within Nature (Oates 2008: 10, 18).

Wain (2007: 1) describes "the invasion of misguided targets and measurement in conservation, and the associated vacuous management culture which can sever the link with real wildlife and real places." Instead, he recommends an alternative discourse:

> Cue another recent book which makes the real thing vivid—Jim Crumley's *Brother Nature*. Crumley takes us up-close to ospreys, kites, wild swans, beavers, and even bears. He reveals the savage beauty of nature in the landscapes of his beloved Highland edge.

Another conservationist, Evans (1996), pinpoints the difference between the discourses of mainstream conservation and alternative, poetic, discourses:

Many conservationists prefer to hide behind the language of science. But why should we be scared of poetic description? Why should we not be concerned with the specific, the individual, the particular and the spirit of place. . . . Nature will not be confined to the abstractions, theories, data sets, computer models and species lists of the nerds — and neither should we (1996: 11).

Russell (2007: 17) is similarly critical of the discourse of mainstream conservation:

The way that we frame our understanding of science, of nature and ac-countability seduces us into dull compliance with regulation and we risk losing the essential qualities of our care; the quality which nourishes our connectivity with nature and with others and which alone will guide us towards a more sustainable way of living.

These authors are criticizing the internal discourse of conservation for dis-tancing conservationists from the world of nature, for erasing the animals and plants that are the subject of concern. Another important dimension is the role played by the *external* discourses of conservation agencies in influencing how the public relates to nature. Pollock (1996: 3–6) questions the specialist terminology used in these external discourses, claiming that the abstractions typically used cannot reach people:

The public already grasps, in an infinity of marvellous and personal ways, the nature of Nature. . . . Yet government, scientists and other professionals continue to talk of *biodiversity*, of *sustainability*, of *not entail-ing excessive cost*. A discourse draining away personal meaning in favour of corporate blandspeak. A language fit for blandscapes, blighted by what Paul Evens dubbed *corporate scrub*. . . . Direct experience of Nature remains the lifeblood of any environmental concern.

All these conservationists are recognizing the power of discourse to shape human relations with animals and nature, and are calling for new forms of lan-guage that inspire connection. It is, of course, not just conservationists who find their professional life becoming increasingly distant from reality, who feel they are immersed in a world of abstractions, targets, statistics, and simulations — it is something that is impacting people everywhere in a globalized world. Conservationists are, however, the ones most likely to recognize the loss entailed, because it was their original connection with nature that brought them into the profession in the first place.

The conservationists above were writing in the journal *Ecos*, produced by the British Association of Nature Conservationists, an organization with the tag-line "Challenging Conservation." The message of these authors goes far beyond conservation, however, challenging all of us to be critical of discourses that are alienating us from animals and nature, and to seek out alternative discourses that can help us reconnect. The stakes could not be higher. Oates (2007: 22) writes, albeit hyperbolically: "We can and must do better than all this, for the alternative is precipitous extinction resultant from the further severance of the relationship between people and nature that is essential for global existence."

In our engrossment in the symbolic world, animals have been erased, existing now for us more in words, statistics, toys, films, cartoons, zoos, museums, and advertisements than in sensual reality. The consequences of this for the welfare of animals and the future of life-supporting ecosystems on Earth are severe. There are two paths toward remedying this situation, and both are equally necessary. The first is to follow the way of social constructionists and reach into the artificial worlds that we have created, criticizing them and rearranging them in ways that lead to more humane and sustainable ways of behaving. The second is to realize that representation always involves erasure of some kind and, at least occasionally, to break free from the artificial worlds we have created and experience animals for who they are.

Bibliography

Abram, D. (1996). *The spell of the sensuous.* New York: Vintage.

Adams, C. (1993). The feminist traffic in animals. In G. Gaard (ed.), *Ecofeminism: Women, animals, nature* (pp. 195–218). Philadelphia, PA: Temple University Press.

Addiss, S., F. Yamamoto, and A. Yamamoto (1992). *A haiku menagerie: Living creatures in poems and prints.* New York: Weatherhill.

Addiss, S., F. Yamamoto, and A. Yamamoto (1996). *A haiku garden: The four seasons in poems and prints.* New York: Weatherhill.

Aitken, R. (1978). *A Zen wave: Bashō's haiku and Zen.* Washington, DC: Shoemaker and Hoard.

Allen, J. (1951). *As a man thinketh.* New York: Peter Pauper Press.

Andrews, T. (1993). *Enchantment of the faerie realm.* St. Paul, MN: Llewellyn Publications.

Appel, A. (2000). [Letter], *Animals Agenda* (March/April): 8.

Armstrong, P. (2008). *What animals mean in the fiction of modernity.* New York: Routledge.

Baker, S. (2001). *Picturing the beast: Animals, identity and representation.* Chicago: University of Illinois Press.

Barbier, E., J. Burgess, and C. Folke (1994). *Paradise lost? The ecological economics of biodiversity.* London: Earthscan.

Barthes, R. (1972). *Mythologies.* London: Vintage.

Bate, J. (2000). *The song of the Earth.* London: Picador.

Baudrillard, J. (1994). *Simulacra and simulation.* Ann Arbor: University of Michigan Press.

Baydack, R., and H. Campa (1999). Setting the context. In R. Baydack, H. Campa, and J. Haufler (eds.), *Practical Approaches to the Conservation of Biological Diversity* (pp. 3–16). Washington, DC: Island Press.

BBC (2001). Cull Cruelty Cases May be Dropped. BBC online news. 21 May. http://news.bbc.co.uk/1/hi/uk/1342791.stm

Beckerman, W. (1974). *In defence of economic growth*. London: Jonathan Cape.

Beckerman, W. (2002). *A poverty of reason: Sustainable development and economic growth*. New York: Independent Institute.

Belk, R. (1996). Metaphoric relationships with pets. *Society and Animals* 4 (2): 121–46.

Berger, J. (1980). *About looking*. New York: Vintage.

Bergman, C. (2005). Inventing a beast with no body: Radio-telemetry, the marginalization of animals, and the simulation of ecology. *Worldviews* 9 (2): 255–70.

Berry, C., and A. Davison (2001). *Bitter harvest: A call for reform in Scottish aquaculture*. WWF www.wwf.org.uk/filelibrary/pdf/bitterharvest.pdf.

Blyth, R. H. (1995). *The genius of haiku: Readings from R. H. Blyth*. Tokyo: Hokuseido.

Bourke, S., and T. Meppem (2000). Privileged narratives and fictions of consent in environmental discourse. *Local Environment* 5 (3): 299–310.

Bowers, C. (2001). *Educating for eco-justice and community*. Athens: University of Georgia Press.

Bowers, F. (1996). *The classic tradition of haiku*. New York: Dover.

Boyd, J., and T. Nishimura (2004). Shinto perspectives in Miyazaki's anime film *Spirited Away*. *Journal of Religion and Film* 8 (2). http://avalon.unomaha.edu/jrf/Vol8No2/boydShinto.htm.

Brazier, D. (1997). *Zen therapy: Transcending the sorrows of the human mind*. New York: Wiley.

Britton, D. (trans.) (1974). *A haiku journey: Bashō's narrow road to a far province*. Tokyo: Kodansha.

Burt, J. (2005). John Berger's *Why Look at Animals?* A Close Reading. *Worldviews: Global Religions, Culture, and Ecology* 9 (2): 203–18.

Butler, J. (2002). Wild salmonids and sea louse infestations on the west coast of Scotland: Sources of infection and implications for the management of marine salmon farms. *Pest Management Science* 58 (6): 595–608.

Calarco, M. (2008). *Zoographies: The question of the animal from Heidegger to Derrida*. New York: Columbia University Press.

Cameron, D. (1995). *Verbal hygiene*. London: Routledge.

Capone D., D. Weston, V. Miller, and C. Shoemaker (1996). Antibacterial residues in marine sediments and invertebrates following chemotherapy in aquaculture. *Aquaculture* 145 (1): 55–75.

Capra, F. (1997) *The web of life: A new scientific understanding of living systems*. New York: Anchor.

Capra, F. (2002). *The hidden connections: A science for sustainable living.* New York: HarperCollins.

Capra, F. (2005). How nature sustains the web of life. In M. Stone and Z. Barlow (eds.), *Ecological literacy: Educating our children for a sustainable world* (pp. xiii–xv). San Francisco: Sierra Club.

Carson, R. (1962). *Silent spring.* Harmondsworth, UK: Penguin.

Carson, R. (1998/1956). *A sense of wonder.* New York: HarperCollins.

Carson, R. (1999/1955). *The edge of the sea.* Gloucester, MA: Peter Smith.

Carson, R. (2003/1951). *The sea around us.* Oxford: Oxford University Press.

Carter, R. (2001). *Encounter with enlightenment: A study of Japanese ethics.* Albany: State University of New York Press.

Chilton, P., and C. Schäffner (1997). Discourse and politics. In Teun van Dijk (ed.), *Discourse as Social Interaction* (pp. 206–30). London: Sage.

Chouliaraki, L., and N. Fairclough (1999). *Discourse in late modernity.* Edinburgh: Edinburgh University Press.

Chuang Tzu (2001). *Teachings and sayings of Chuang Tzu.* New York: Dover.

Clinebell, H. (1996). *Ecotherapy: Healing ourselves, healing the Earth.* New York: Routledge.

Coats, D. (1989). *Old MacDonald's factory farm.* New York: Continuum.

Conn, S. (1995). When the Earth hurts, who responds? In A. Kanner, T. Roszak, and M. Gomes (eds.), *Ecopsychology: Restoring the Earth, healing the mind* (pp. 156–82). New York: Sierra Club Books.

Cooper, D. (1992). The idea of environment. In D. Cooper and J. Palmer (eds.), *The Environment in Question.* London: Routledge.

Cooper, N. (2000). Speaking and listening to nature: Ethics within ecology. *Biodiversity and Conservation* 9: 1009–27.

Crow, L. (1996). Including all of our lives: Renewing the social model of disability. In C. Barnes and G. Mercer (eds.), *Exploring the Divide* (pp. 55–72). Leeds, UK: The Disability Press.

Daly, H., and J. Farley (2004). *Ecological economics: Principles and applications.* Washington, DC: Island Press.

Danto, A. (1987). *Mysticism and morality: Oriental thought and moral philosophy.* New York: Harper and Row.

Davies, I., and G. Rodger (2000). A review of the use of ivermectin as a treatment for sea lice infestation in farmed Atlantic salmon. *Aquaculture Research* 31 (11): 869–83.

Delong, D. (1996). Defining biodiversity. *Wildlife Society Bulletin* 24 (4): 738–49.

Dendrinos, B. (1992). *The EFL textbook and ideology*. Athens, Greece: Grivas.

Dentith, S. (1995) *Bakhtin thought: An introductory reader*. London: Routledge.

Deutsch, S. (2005) Smithfield draws mixed reviews in Poland. *National Hog Farmer*. http://nationalhogfarmer.com/mag/farming_smithfield_draws_mixed

Devall, B., and G. Sessions (1985). *Deep ecology: Living as if nature mattered*. Salt Lake City, UT: Gibbs Smith.

Diesendorf, M., and C. Hamilton (1997). *Human ecology, human economy: Towards an ecologically sustainable society*. St. Leonards, NSW, Australia: Allen & Unwin.

Disney (2006). *My neighbor Totoro*. Directed by Miyazaki Hayao. DVD, English dubbing. New York: Walt Disney.

Donaldson, A. (2001). Q & A: Foot-and-mouth disease. *Times* (London), February 21.

Donovan, J. (1993). Animal rights and feminist theory. In G. Gaard (ed.) *Ecofeminism: Women, animals, nature* (pp. 167–94). Philadelphia, PA: Temple University Press.

Dunayer, J. (2001). *Animal equality: Language and liberation*. Derwood, MD: Ryce.

Earth Charter (2005). The Earth Charter. www.earthcharterinaction.org/content/pages/Read-the-Charter.html.

Eccleston, P. (2007). Red list of endangered species. *Telegraph*, September 12.

Ecological Society of America (1997). Ecosystem services: Benefits supplied to human societies by natural ecosystems. *Issues in Ecology* 2 (Spring).

Eisnitz, Gail (1997). *Slaughterhouse: The shocking story of greed, neglect, and inhumane treatment inside the U.S. meat industry*. New York: Prometheus.

Ekins, P., M. Hillman, and R. Hutchinson (1992). *Wealth beyond measure: An atlas of new economics*. London: Gaia.

Evans, P. (1996). Biodiversity: Nature for nerds? *ECOS: A Review of Conservation* 17 (2): 7–11.

Fairclough, N. (1989). *Language and Power*. London: Longman.

Fairclough, N. (1992a). *Critical Language Awareness*. London: Longman.

Fairclough, N. (1992b). *Discourse and Social Change*. Cambridge, UK: Polity Press.

Fairclough, N. (1999). Global Capitalism and Critical Awareness of Language. *Language Awareness* 8 (2): 71–83.

Fairclough, N. (2003a). *Analysing Discourse: Textual analysis for social research*. London: Routledge.

Fairclough, N. (2003b). "Political correctness": The politics of culture and language. *Discourse & Society* 14 (1): 17–28.

Fiddes, N. (1991). *Meat, a natural symbol.* London: Routledge.

Field (2008). Biodiversity and conservation: The web of life. *The Field Museum.* www .fieldmuseum.org/biodiversity/intro.html.

Fowler, R. (1991). *Language in the news: Discourse and ideology in the press.* London: Routledge.

Fox (1993). *My neighbor Totoro.* Directed by Miyazaki Hayao. DVD, English dubbing. New York: Fox.

Franklin, S. (2007). *Dolly mixtures: The remaking of genealogy.* London: Duke University Press.

Freedland, J. (2001). Special report: Foot and mouth disease. *Guardian,* May 16.

Freeman, C. (2009). This little piggy went to press: The American news media's construction of animals in agriculture. *Communication Review* 12: 78–103.

Garner, R. (1998). Defending animal rights. *Parliamentary Affairs* 51 (3): 458–69.

Gazdar, G. (1978). *Pragmatics: Implicative, presupposition, and logical form.* New York: Academic Press.

Gergen, K. (1999). *An invitation to social construction.* London: Sage.

Gergen, K. (2000). Interview *PMTH NEWS,* May 11. http://users.rcn.com/rathbone/ pm051100.htm.

Ghibli (1988). *Tonari no Totoro.* Directed by Miyazaki Hayao. DVD, Japanese release. Tokyo: Ghibli Studios.

Glenn C. (2004). Constructing consumables and consent: A critical analysis of factory farm industry discourse. *Journal of Communication Inquiry* 28 (1): 63–81.

Goatly, A. (2000). *Critical reading and writing: An introductory coursebook.* London: Routledge.

Goatly, A. (2006). Humans, animals and metaphors. *Society and Animals* 14 (1): 15–37.

Gold, M. (1995). *Animal rights: Extending the circle of compassion.* Oxford: Jon Carpenter.

Grumbine, E. (1992). *Ghost bears: Exploring the biodiversity crisis.* Washington, DC: Island Press.

Hagen, S. (1999). *Buddhism Plain and Simple.* New York: Arkana.

Haila, Y. (1999). Biodiversity and the divide between culture and nature. *Biodiversity and Conservation* 8: 165–81.

Hails, C. (2007). The evolution of approaches to conserving the world's natural heritage: The experiences of WWF. *International Journal of Heritage Studies* 13 (4–5): 365–79.

Halffter, G. (2002). Conservación de la Biodiversidad en el Siglo XXI. *Aracnet* 10 (31): 1–7.

Halffter, G. (2005). Towards a culture of biodiversity conservation. *Acta Zoológica Mexicana* 21 (2): 133–53.

Hall, S. (1997). *Representation: Cultural representations and signifying practices*. London: Sage.

Halliday, M. (2001). New ways of meaning: The challenge to applied linguistics. In A. Fill and P. Mühlhäusler (eds.), *The ecolingusitics reader* (pp. 175–202). London: Continuum.

Halliday, M. (2004). *An introduction to functional grammar*. 3rd ed. London: Hodder Arnold.

Harada, S. (1993). *The essence of Zen*. Tokyo: Kodansha.

Haraway, D. (1989). *Primate visions: Gender, race and nature in the world of modern science*. New York: Routledge.

Harnack, A. (ed.) (1996). *Animal rights: Opposing viewpoints*. San Diego, CA: Greenhaven Press.

Hawksworth, D. (1995). *Biodiversity: Measurement and estimation*. London: Chapman and Hall.

Hedgepeth, W. (1998). *The hog book*. 2nd ed. Athens: University of Georgia Press.

Hellsten, I. (2002). *The politics of metaphor: Biotechnology and biodiversity in the media*. Academic dissertation. University of Tampere, Finland.

Henderson, H. (1958). *An introduction to haiku: An anthology of poems and poets from Bashō to Shiki*. New York: Doubleday Anchor.

Henning, D. (2002). *Buddhism and deep ecology*. Bloomington, IN: 1stBooks.

Herrick, J. (1995). Food for thought for food animal veterinarians. *Journal of the American Veterinary Medical Association* 207 (8): 1031–36.

Higginson, W. (1996). *The haiku seasons: Poetry of the natural world*. Tokyo: Kodansha.

Highfield, R. (2007). Extinction in the wild is "danger to humans." *Telegraph*, July 12.

Hirashima, N. (1997). Fantashi ga umareru kukan [The space where fantasy is born]. *Eureka* 29 (11): 164–69

Hoard's Dairyman. (1995). Animal rights, animal welfare and you. *Hoard's Dairyman* 140 (11): 449

Hodge, R., and G. Kress (1993), *Language as ideology*. 2nd ed. London: Routledge.

Ishizawa, J., and E. Fernández (2002). Loving the world as it is: Western abstraction and Andean nurturance. *ReVision* 24 (4): 21–24.

Jacobs, G., and A. Goatly (2000). The treatment of ecological issues in ELT coursebooks. *ELT Journal* 54 (3): 256–64.

James, S. (2003). Zen Buddhism and the intrinsic value of nature. *Contemporary Buddhism* 4 (2): 143–57.

James, S. (2004). *Zen Buddhism and environmental ethics*. London: Ashgate.

Jepson, J. (2008). A linguistic analysis of discourse on the killing of nonhuman animals. *Society and Animals* 16: 127–48.

Johnson, M. (1983). Metaphorical reasoning. *Southern Journal of Philosophy* 21 (3): 371–89.

Jones, A., and J. O'Neil (2002). *Seasons of grace: The life-giving practice of gratitude*. London: Wiley.

Jones, D. (1997). The media's response to animal rights activism. *Anthrozoös* 10 (2–3): 67–75.

Juniper, A. (2003). *Wabi-sabi: The Japanese art of impermanence*. Clarendon, VT: Tuttle.

Kadmon, N. (2000). *Formal Pragmatics: Semantics, Pragmatics, Presupposition, and Focus*. London: Blackwell.

Kalland, A. (2002). Holism and sustainability: Lessons from Japan. *Worldviews* 6 (2): 145–58.

Kanner, A., T. Roszak, and M. Gomes (eds.) (1995). *Ecopsychology: Restoring the Earth, healing the mind*. New York: Sierra Club Books.

Kanō, S. (1998). *Tonari no Totoro no shizenkan* [The representation of nature in *Tonari no Totoro*]. www.yk.rim.or.jp/~rst/rabo/miyazaki/totoro_i.html.

Kareiva, P., and M. Marvier (2003). Conserving biodiversity coldspots. *American Scientist* 91 (July–August): 344–51.

Kerr, A. (2002). *Dogs and demons: Tales from the dark side of modern Japan*. New York: Hill and Wang.

Kettlewell, J. (2004) "Frozen ark" to save animal DNA. BBC *News online*. http://news.bbc.co.uk/1/hi/sci/tech/3928411.stm.

Kheel, M. (1995). License to kill: An ecofeminist critique of hunters' discourse. In C. Adams and J. Donovan (eds.), *Animals and women: Feminist theoretical explanations* (pp. 85–125). Durham, NC: Duke University Press.

Kibenge, F, K. Munir, M. Kibenge, T. Joseph, and E. Moneke (2004). Infectious salmon anemia virus: Causative agent, pathogenesis and immunity. *Animal Health Research Reviews* 5 (1): 65–78.

Kiridōshi, R. (2001). *Miyazaki Hayao no sekai* [The world of Miyazaki Hayao] Tokyo: Chikuma Shobou.

Kopperud, S. (1993). What's animal agriculture doing about animal rights? *Agricultural Engineering* (May): 20–22.

Krech, G. (2002). *Naikan: Gratitude, grace and the Japanese art of self-reflection*. Berkeley, CA: Stone Bridge Press.

Kress, G., and T. van Leeuwen (1996). *Reading images: The grammar of visual design*. London: Routledge.

Lakoff, G. (1987) *Women, fire and dangerous things: What categories reveal about the mind*. Chicago: University of Chicago Press.

Lakoff, G. (1991). Metaphor and war: The metaphor system used to justify war in the Gulf. In B. Hallet (ed.), *Engulfed in war: Just war and the Persian Gulf*. Honolulu, HI: Matsunaga Institute for Peace.

Lakoff, G., and M. Johnson (1980). *Metaphors we live by*. Chicago: University of Chicago Press.

Lakoff, G., and M. Johnson (1999). *Philosophy in the flesh: The embodied mind and its challenge to Western thought*. New York: Basic Books.

Lamarre, T. (2002). From animation to anime: Drawing movements and moving drawings. *Japan Forum* 14 (2): 329–67.

Lanoue, D. (2006). *Haiku of Kobayashi Issa*. www.haikuguy.com/issa.

Lawrence, E. (1994). Conflicting ideologies: Views of animal rights advocates and their opponents. *Society and Animals* 2 (2): 175–90.

Leach, E. (1964). Anthropological aspects of language: Animal categories and verbal abuse. In E. Lenneberg (ed.), *New directions in the study of language*. Cambridge, MA: MIT Press.

Leopold, A. (1966). *A Sand County almanac*. New York: Ballantine.

Light, A., and H. Rolston (2003). *Environmental ethics: An anthology*. London: Blackwell.

Lomborg, B. (2001). *The sceptical environmentalist: Measuring the real state of the world*. Cambridge, MA: Cambridge University Press.

Loy, D. (1998). Loving the world as our own body: The nondualist ethics of Taoism, Buddhism and deep ecology. In Carl Becker (ed.), *Asian and Jungian views of ethics* (pp. 85–112). Westport, CT: Greenwood

Luke, T. (2002). Deep ecology: Living as if nature mattered: Devall and Sessions on defending the Earth. *Organization & Environment* 15 (2): 178–86.

MacGarvin, M. (2000) Scotland's secret? Aquaculture, nutrient pollution eutrophication and toxic blooms. *Modus Vivendi*, WWF Scotland (September). www.wwf.org .uk/filelibrary/pdf/secret.pdf.

Mackenzie, L. (1957). *The autumn wind: A selection from the poems of Issa*. Tokyo: Kodansha.

Malamud, R. (1998). *Reading zoos: Representations of animals and captivity*. New York: New York University Press.

Malcolmson, R., and B. Mastoris (1998). *The English pig: A history*. London: Hambledon and London.

Manes, C. (1990). *Green rage: Radical environmentalism and the unmaking of civilization*. New York: Little, Brown and Company.

Marcus, E. (1998). *Vegan: The new ethics of eating*. Ithaca, NY: McBooks Press.

Martens, P., J. Rotmans, and D. de Groot (2003). Biodiversity: Luxury or necessity? *Global Environmental Change* 13: 75–81.

Max-Neef, M. (1992). Development and human needs. In P. Ekins and M. Max-Neef (eds.), *Real-life economics: Understanding wealth creation* (pp. 197–213). London: Routledge.

McCarthy, H. (1999). *Hayao Miyazaki: Master of Japanese animation*. Berkeley, CA: Stone Bridge Press.

McIntosh, A. (2001). *Soil and soul: People versus corporate power*. London: Aurum.

McNeill, J. (2000). *Something new under the sun*. New York: Norton.

Meat Marketing & Technology (1995). Proper treatment of hogs prior to stunning. http://mtgplace.com/articles/m3.asp.

Metrick, A. and M. Weitzman (1998) Conflicts and choices in biodiversity preservation. *Journal of Economic Perspectives* 12:3:21–34

Millennium Ecosystem Assessment (2005). *Ecosystems and human well-being: Synthesis*. Washington, DC: Island Press.

Miller, K, J. Winton, A. Schulze, M. Purcell, and T. Ming (2004). Major histocompatibility complex loci are associated with susceptibility of Atlantic salmon to infectious hematopoietic necrosis virus. *Environmental Biology of Fishes* 69 (1–4): 307–16.

Miller, T. (1999) *Environmental Science*. London: Wadsworth.

Miller, T. (2002). *Sustaining the earth: An integrated approach*. London: Wadsworth.

Mills, S. (2003). Caught between sexism, anti-sexism and "political correctness": Feminist women's negations with naming practices. *Discourse & Society* 14 (1): 87–110.

Miura, Y. (1991). *Classic haiku: A master's selection*. Tokyo: Tuttle.

Miyazaki, H. (1988). Interview with Miyazaki Hayao. *Tonari no Totoro*. Directed by Miyazaki Hayao. DVD, Japanese release. Tokyo: Ghibli.

Monbiot, G. (2000). The more we spend, the happier we become. Probably. *Guardian*, December 28.

Monbiot, G. (2004a). Natural aesthetes. *Guardian*, January 13.

Monbiot, G. (2004b). No longer obeying orders. *Monbiot.com*. www.monbiot.com/ archives/2004/10/06/no-longer-obeying-orders.

Naess, A. (1973). The shallow and the deep, long-range ecology movements: A summary. *Inquiry* 16: 95–100.

Naess, A. (1990). *Ecology, community and lifestyle: Outline of an Ecosophy*. Cambridge, MA: Cambridge University Press.

Napier, S. (2001). Confronting master narratives: History as vision in Miyazaki Hayao's cinema of de-assurance. *Positions* 9 (2): 467–93.

Newman, J. (2009). Values reflection and the Earth Charter. In Arran Stibbe (ed.), *The handbook of sustainability literacy: Skills for a changing world* (pp. 99–104). Dartington, UK: Green Books.

Oates, M. (2007). The soul within. *ECOS: A Review of Conservation* 28 (1): 19–26.

Oates, M. (2008). Obfuscation and the language of nature conservation. *ECOS: A Review of Conservation* 29 (1): 10–18.

Odin, S. (1997). The Japanese Concept of Nature in Relation to the Environmental Ethics and Conservation Aesthetics of Aldo Leopold. In M. Tucker and D. Williams (eds.), *Buddhism and Ecology* (pp. 89–110). Cambridge, MA: Harvard University Press.

Odum, E. (1997). *Ecology: A bridge between science and society*. Sunderland, MA: Sinauer Associates.

Okakura, K. (1956). *The book of tea*. Tokyo: Tuttle.

Olson, C. (2000). *Zen and the art of postmodern philosophy*. Albany: State University of New York Press.

O'Neill, J. (1993). *Ecology, policy, politics*. London: Routledge.

Ong, W. (2002). *Oralcy and literacy*. London: Routledge.

Ooka, M. (1997). *The poetry and poetics of ancient Japan*. Honolulu, HI: Katydid books.

Orr, D. (1992). *Ecological literacy: Education and the transition to a postmodern world*. Albany: State University of New York Press.

Ott, R. (1995). The natural wrongs about animal rights and animal liberation. *Journal of the American Veterinary Medical Association* 207 (8): 1023–30.

Palmatier, R. (1995). *Speaking of animals: A dictionary of animal metaphors*. Westport, CT: Greenwood Press.

Pearce, F. (2007). Britain fails to protect its overseas biodiversity. *Telegraph*, October 3.

Peeler, E., and A. Murray (2004). Disease interaction between farmed and wild fish populations, *Journal of Fish Biology* 65 (1): 321–22.

Pennycook, A. (1998). *English and the discourses of colonialism*. London: Routledge.

Phillipson, R. (1992). *Linguistic imperialism*. Oxford: Oxford University Press.

Philo, C., and C. Wilbert (2000). *Animal spaces, beastly places: New geographies of human-animal relations*. London: Routledge.

Pickett, S., and M. Cadenasso (2002). The ecosystem as a multidimensional concept: Meaning, model and metaphor. *Ecosystems* 5: 1–10.

PIH (*Pork Industry Handbook*) (2002). CD-ROM edition. Lafayette, IN: Purdue University Press. (NB: Numbers in citations refer to information sheet numbers rather than page numbers.)

PIH (*Pork Industry Handbook*) (2003). Information brochure L233. www.ansi.okstate.edu/exten/swine/L-223.PDF.

Plumwood, V. (2003). Animals and ecology: Towards a better integration. Unpublished paper. http://socpol.anu.edu.au/pdf-files/Vegpap6%20%20.pdf.

Pollock, J. (1996). Negative science, positive public: A Jeremiad on "biodiversion." *ECOS: A Review of Conservation* 17 (2): 2–6.

Potter, J. (1996). *Representing reality: Discourse, rhetoric and social construction*. London: Sage.

Poultry magazine. (1995). Salmonella is scarce in Sweden. http://mtgplace.com/articles/p347.asp.

Poultry magazine. (1997a). Lowering catching stress — automatic broiler harvesters. http://mtgplace.com/articles/p913.asp.

Poultry magazine. (1997b). Recent success with gas stunning in Brazil perks up the ears of U.S. processors. http://mtgplace.com/articles/p927.asp.

Price, S. (2001). Cartoons from another planet: Japanese animation as cross-cultural communication. *Journal of American and Comparative Cultures* 24 (1–2): 153–69.

Regan, T. (1985). The case for animal rights. In P. Singer (ed.), *In defence of animals* (pp. 13–26). New York: Basil Blackwell.

Regan, T. (1996). The case for strong animal rights. In A. Harnack (ed.), *Animal rights: Opposing viewpoints* (pp. 34–40). San Diego, CA: Greenhaven Press.

Rigby, C. (2001). *What are poets for? Heidegger's gift to eco-criticism*. Centre for Comparative Literature and Cultural Studies, Monash University. www.arts.monash.edu.au/cclcs/research/papers/assets/Heidegger.pdf

Rogers, C. (1961). *On becoming a person: A therapist's view of psychotherapy*. Boston: Houghton Mifflin.

Rosch, E. (1975). Cognitive representations of semantic categories. *Journal of Experimental Psychology: General* 104: 193–233.

Rosch, E. (1981) Prototype classification and logical classification: The two systems. In E. Scholnick (ed.), *New trends in cognitive representation: Challenges to Piaget's theory* (pp. 73–86). Hillsdale, NJ: Erlbaum.

Roszak, T., M. Gomes, and A. Kanner (1995). *Ecopsychology: Restoring the Earth, healing the mind*. Berkley: University of California Press.

Royal Society (2002). *Infectious diseases in livestock*. http://royalsociety.org/inquiry/index.html.

Russell, D. (2007). Riding the managerial tiger: Risk, accountability and being human. *ECOS: A Review of Conservation* 28 (1): 11–18.

Saito, Y. (1992). The Japanese love of nature: a paradox. *Landscape* 31 (2): 1–8.

Scarce, R. (1997). Socially constructing Pacific salmon. *Society and Animals* 5 (2): 117–35.

Scarce, R. (2000). *Fishy business: Salmon, biology, and the social constructions of nature*. Philadelphia: Temple University Press.

Schank, R., and R. Abelson (1977). *Scripts, plans, goals and understanding*. Hillsdale, NJ: Erlbaum.

Schillo, K. (2003). Critical perspectives of animal agriculture: Introduction. *Journal of Animal Science* 81: 2880–86.

Sustainable Development Commission (2005). *Sustainable Development Commission: Our work, our principles*. www.sd-commission.org.uk/pages/our_work/our_principles.html.

Sen, S. (1979). *Tea life, tea mind*. Tokyo: Weatherhill.

Shapiro, K. (1995). The caring sleuth: A qualitative analysis of animal rights activists. *Alternative Methods in Toxicology* 11: 669–74.

Shepard, P. (1995). Nature and madness. In T. Roszak, M. Gomes, and A. Kanner (eds.), *Ecopsychology: Restoring the Earth, healing the mind* (pp. 21–40). Berkley: University of California Press.

Shimizu, M. (1997). Sukoyakanaru mōsō [The quieting of the imagination]. *Pop Culture Critique* 1: 92–101.

Shiva, V. (2001). Unholy mess. *Guardian*, April 4.

Shotter, J. (1993). *Conversational realities: Constructing life through language*. London: Sage.

Singer, P. (1985). Ethics and the new animal liberation movement. In P. Singer (ed.), *In defence of animals* (pp. 1–12). New York: Basil Blackwell.

Singer, P. (1990/1975). *Animal liberation*. 2nd ed. New York: New York Review.

Singer, P. (2003). Animal liberation at 30. *New York Review of Books* 50: 8. www.nybooks
.com/articles/16276.

Smith, G., and D. Williams (eds.) (1999). *Ecological education in action: On weaving education, culture and the environment.* Albany: State University of New York Press.

Smith-Harris, T. (2004). There's not enough and there's no sense: Language usage and human perceptions of other animals. *Revision* 27 (2): 12–15.

Snyder, G. (2000). Language goes two ways. In C. McEwan and M. Statman (eds.), *The alphabet of the trees: A guide to nature writing.* New York: Philmark Lithographics.

Spender, D. (1998). *Man made language.* New York: Rivers Oram.

Sperling, S. (1988). *Animal liberators: Research and morality.* Berkeley: University of California Press.

Scottish Quality Salmon (2005). *Scottish Quality Salmon: The Facts.* Perth: Scottish Quality Salmon.

Stamos, D. (2003). *The Species Concept: Biological Species, Ontology, and the Metaphysics of Biology.* Lanham, MD: Lexington.

Staniford, D. (2002). Sea cage fish farming: An evaluation of environmental and public health aspects. Paper presented at the European Parliament on October 1, 2002. www.europarl.eu.int/hearings/20021001/pech/programme_en.pdf

Stedman-Edwards, P. (2001). A framework for analysing biodiversity loss. In M. Heemskerk, A. Wood, P. Stedman-Edwards, and J. Mang (eds.), *The root causes of biodiversity loss.* London: World Wildlife Fund and Earthscan.

Stephens, A., and A. Cooper (2004). Ecological model of interactions between escaped and wild Atlantic salmon Salmo salar. *Journal of Fish Biology* 65 (1): 323–23.

Sterling, S. (2001). *Sustainable Education: Re-visioning Learning and Change.* Dartington, UK: Green Books.

Stibbe, A. (2005a). Abracadabra, alakazam: Colonialism and the discourse of entertainment magic. *Soundings* 88 (3–4): 413–26.

Stibbe, A. (2005b). Chance encounters: Ecology and haiku-inspired photography. *Language and Ecology* 1 (4). www.ecoling.net/haikuphotography.html.

Stibbe, A. (2009). Ecolinguistics and Globalisation. In N. Coupland (ed.), *Blackwell handbook of language and globalisation.* London: Blackwell.

Stone, E. (1999). Modern slogan, ancient script: Impairment and disability in the Chinese language. In M. Corker and S. French (eds.), *Disability discourse* (pp.136–47). Buckingham, UK: Open University Press.

Stone, M., and Z. Barlow (eds.) (2005). *Ecological literacy: Educating our children for a sustainable world* (pp. xiii–xv). San Francisco: Sierra Club Books.

Stott, P. (2002). "Sustainable development" is just dangerous nonsense. *Telegraph*, August 16.

Stryk, L. (1985). *On love and barley: Haiku of Bashō*. Honolulu: University of Hawaii Press.

Suzuki, D. T. (1970). *Zen and Japanese culture*. Princeton, NJ: Princeton University Press.

Takacs, D. (1996). *The idea of biodiversity: Philosophies of paradise*. Baltimore: Johns Hopkins University Press.

Taylor, B. (2007). Exploring religion, nature, and culture. *Journal for the Study of Religion, Nature and Culture* 1 (1): 5–23.

Tester, K. (1991). *Animals and society: The humanity of animal rights*. London: Routledge.

Toften H., and M. Jobling (1996). Development of spinal deformities in Atlantic salmon and Arctic charr fed diets supplemented with oxytetracycline. *Journal of Fish Biology* 49 (4): 668–77.

Turner, J. (1999). *Factory farming and the environment*. Hampshire, UK: Compassion in World Farming Trust.

Ueda, M. (1982). *Matsuo Bashō*. Tokyo: Kodansha.

Ueda, M. (2003). *Far beyond the field: Haiku by Japanese women*. New York: Columbia University Press.

UNESCO (2005). Convention on Biological Diversity. www.cbd.int/convention/articles.shtml?a=cbd-02.

Valentine, J. (1998). Naming the other: Power, politeness and the inflation of euphemisms. *Sociological Research Online* 3 (4). www.socresonline.org.uk/3/4/7.html

Väliverronen, E. (1998). Biodiversity and the power of metaphor in environmental discourse. *Science Studies* 11 (1): 19–34.

Väliverronen, E., and I. Hellsten (2002). From "burning library" to "green medicine": The role of metaphors in communicating biodiversity. *Science Communication* 24 (2): 229–45.

Van Dijk, T. (1988). *News as Discourse*. Hillsdale, NJ: Erlbaum.

Van Dijk, T. (1993). Principles of critical discourse analysis. *Discourse and Society* 4 (2): 249–83.

Van Dijk, T. (1997). Discourse as interaction in society. In T. van Dijk (ed.), *Discourse as Social Interaction* (pp. 1–37). London: Sage.

Van Dijk, T. (ed.) (2000). Aims and scope. *Discourse and Society* 11 (4): back cover.

Wain, G. (2007). Feral feelings. *ECOS: A Review of Conservation* 28 (2): 1

Wildlife (2007). 25 ways to get wildlife into your garden. *Telegraph*, September 7.

Wilson, E. (1992). *The diversity of life*. Harmondsworth, UK: Penguin.

Wood, A., P. Stedman-Edwards, and J. Mang (eds.) (2000). *The root causes of biodiversity loss*. London: Earthscan.

Wood, I. (2007). Orangutan project offers hope in Borneo. *Telegraph*, October 22.

WWF-Global (2010). The World Wide Fund for Nature. www.wwf.org.

WWF-UK (2010). The World Wide Fund for Nature. www.wwf.org.uk.

WWF-USA (2010). The World Wide Fund for Nature. www.worldwildlife.org/species.

Yencken, D. (2000). Attitudes to Nature in the East and West. In D. Yencken, J. Fien, and H. Sykes (eds.), *Environment, education and society in the Asia-Pacific: Local traditions and global discourses*. London: Routledge.

Yuasa, N. (1967). *The narrow road to the deep north and other travel sketches by Matsuo Bashō*. Harmondsworth, UK: Penguin.

Index

About the Author

Arran Stibbe has an academic background in both linguistics and human ecology, and combines the two in his teaching and research in the area of ecolinguistics. He is a Reader in Ecological Linguistics at the University of Gloucestershire and a holder of a National Teaching Fellowship in recognition of excellence in teaching. Dr. Stibbe is the founder of the *Language and Ecology Research Forum* (www.ecoling.net) and editor of the journal *Language and Ecology*, and a convenor of the Sustainability in Higher Education Developers (SHED) group. In 2009 he edited *The Handbook of Sustainability Literacy: Skills for a Changing World*, which takes a multidisciplinary look at the skills that people need for surviving and thriving in the twenty-first century (www.sustainability-literacy.org).